Nan̄_____ P9-BYB-007

CONFRONTING

THE

VICTIM ROLE

Also by Barry and Emily McCarthy available from Carroll & Graf:

Couple Sexual Awareness
Female Sexual Awareness
Intimate Marriage
Male Sexual Awareness by Barry McCarthy
Sexual Awareness

Confronting the Victim Role

The

Victim Role

Healing from an Abusive Childhood

Barry and Emily McCarthy

Carroll & Graf Publishers, Inc.
New York

Copyright © 1993 by Barry and Emily McCarthy

All rights reserved

First Carroll & Graf edition 1993

Carroll & Graf Publishers, Inc.
260 Fifth Avenue
New York, NY 10001

Library of Congress Cataloging-in-Publication Data

McCarthy, Barry W., 1943–
    Confronting the victim role : healing from an abusive childhood /
Barry and Emily McCarthy. — 1st ed.
        p.   cm.
    ISBN 0-7867-0011-4 : $11.95
    1. Adult child abuse victims—Psychology.   I. McCarthy, Emily J.
II. Title.
HV6626.5.M386   1993
362.7′64—dc20   93-26371
                                                                              CIP

Manufactured in the United States of America

CONTENTS

Part I—Dealing With the Past

1.	The Pendulum: From Denial to Definition	9
2.	Defining Yourself as a Victim	25
3.	Family of Origin: Dysfunction and Strengths	40
4.	Growing Up in an Alcoholic Family	53
5.	Spouse and Child Abuse	68
6.	Incest: The Shameful Family Secret	83
7.	Dangers of Parent Bashing	98
8.	Accepting the Reality of Your Childhood	111

Part II—Present and Future

9.	The Victim Cycle	127
10.	Co-Dependence—An Overused Concept	142
11.	Twelve-Step Groups	156
12.	Pop Psychology Gurus vs. Psychotherapy	172
13.	Being a Survivor—Living in the Present	187
14.	Psychological Well-Being	203

Appendix I—Choosing a Therapist and Self-Help Group
217

Appendix II—Books for Further Reading   221

I
DEALING WITH THE PAST

1
THE PENDULUM:
FROM DENIAL TO DEFINITION

Denial of physical and sexual abuse in families has led to tragedy. The past decade has witnessed an outpouring of first-person tales, books about abuse, 12-step groups, and talk show discussions of traumatized childhoods. Adult Children of Alcoholics is the largest of these self-help movements, but there are over thirty such groups, including Adult Children of Dysfunctional Families, Incest Survivors, Adults Battered as Children, Adult Children of Divorce. Has the pendulum swung too far? Have we gone from the extreme of denial and cover-up to the extreme of identification as a victim? Is childhood trauma the primary cause of adult problems? Is it healthy to be defined as an adult child? Is "finding the child within and loving her" really the prime task of adulthood? Are over 90% of families dysfunctional? Are 97% of people co-dependent? Are 12-step programs the only road to recovery?

This book will address these multifaceted, complex issues with the respect they deserve. For adults who grew up in abusive or dysfunctional families, developing self-esteem and a healthy family of creation is of prime importance. They need more than clichés from magazine articles, books, and talk shows. Adults have to accept the reality of their childhood (with its positives as well as negatives), but not allow the sense of victimization to control self-esteem. Without it becoming a substitute cliché, the central theme of this book is learning to be a survivor who leads a responsible, satisfying life. In clinical work with rape victims, a favorite saying is, "Living well is the best revenge." This is equally applicable for adults from dysfunctional families.

The worst mistake is to retreat behind the wall of denial and minimization. The reality of alcoholism, family violence, sexual abuse, and emotional neglect cannot be denied. Whether caused by poverty, depression, stress, anger, lack of life skills, alcohol or drug abuse, or mental illness, parental abuse can brutally traumatize the child. Dysfunction increases when the child keeps these problems secret. As an adult, the secrets become larger and more distorted with self-blame, shame, and guilt. No, the pendulum cannot return to denial and avoidance. Awareness of abuse and trauma is necessary for individuals, families, and the culture.

People receive great benefit from breaking the conspiracy of silence. Reading books that contain the message that childhood abuse is not a shameful secret, and has happened to others, is validating. Being in a self-help group where you share the pain of incest, growing up in a violent family, or with an alcoholic parent can be profoundly healing. The 12-step concept of recovery and establishing spiritual meaning has changed the lives of hundreds of thousands of people.

How far has the pendulum swung? Unfortunately, many adults center their lives and self-esteem on childhood abuse and victimization. They spend inordinate time and energy trying to uncover repressed traumatic memories. In the quest to discover and nurture the "child within," they ignore health, jobs, relationships, parenting, and responsibilities. This is self-indulgent and, in the long run, a self-defeating strategy. Those close to the person (especially spouse and children) become disappointed, angry, and lose respect for her. To attain psychological well-being, the person has to establish a balance between dealing with the past and leading her life in a respectful, responsible manner. Obsessively living in the past and feeling victimized by childhood trauma is almost as harmful as denying and avoiding the past.

OUR REALITY FOCUS

This book is not an attack on 12-step programs, self-help groups, or the recovery movement. They have increased awareness, confronted denial, and helped many. What this book does denounce is extremism and simple answers to complex psychological and life issues. Most important, it criticizes the view that there is one answer, one way to approach abusive or dysfunctional problems, and over-promising total cures. The reality of the human condition is life is multicausal, complex, and variable.

Childhood trauma and growing up in a dysfunctional family does have lasting effects. For some people, those effects are profound. For others, relatively benign. Some people's entire childhood was controlled by abuse, whether physical battering, incest, or angry tirades about the child being responsible for wrecking the parent's life. More often, abusive behavior occurred over a period of months or years and abated as circumstances changed—finances improved, a job change, family move, a parent stopped drinking, there was a divorce. The most common pattern is intermittent abuse. Life proceeded relatively well for a time, but the parent became depressed, there were marital fights, Father's drinking became out of control, there were severe financial problems, a grandparent became ill and the parent could not cope. When the crisis abated, the family and parenting improved for a time. The child does not cause family dysfunction nor can he cure it. The child's life, however, is affected by it.

Ideally, every child deserves to grow up in a safe, secure, loving, nurturing family, with no abuse or dysfunction. However, the perfect, problem-free, totally loving childhood is not the reality for *any* child. Whether a broken arm or a broken marriage, a depressed mother or a distant, uninvolved father, a sense of confusion caused by a move, or stifled by an overinvolved extended family, no one has a storybook childhood, nor should they. The most important learning of childhood is preparing to live as an independent, responsible, loving adult who can take care of himself and deal with others. The opposite of an abused childhood is not a picture-perfect childhood. Growing up in a healthy family includes experiencing frustrations and disappointments. Remember, parents are human beings with their own strengths and weaknesses. There are no "perfect parents" any more than there are "perfect children" or "perfect families." The search for the "pure, innocent child within" is as futile as for the "perfect, loving, giving parent." Parents and families are not a dichotomy of either "abusive/dysfunctional" or "loving/nurturing." Rather, growing up is a continuum, with all kinds of gradations and mixtures. A short case vignette will make this point more clearly.

Laurie's Family. Laurie was a twenty-year-old college student who had taken a psychology course, "Human Sexual Behavior." She was an excellent student, receiving As on papers and exams, but quiet in class. A month after the semester, she called her professor, who was also a practicing therapist, and asked if he would see her family in short-term therapy to deal with a specific problem.

In family therapy it is advisable, if possible, to start with the whole family or at least the members directly affected. In this case, it was Laurie, Mother, Stepfather, and older sister, Beth. The stated agenda was to talk about past family difficulties. The tension in the room was palpable. Family therapy conceptualizes problems as involving the entire family while respecting each individual's needs. Each person was given an individual therapy appointment after the initial family session to help understand their perceptions and needs.

Beth was the first seen and stated she was doing this primarily to support Laurie. Beth was ready to separate from the family and establish her life; she was engaged to be married in five months. Mother left Father when Beth was six and

Laurie two, and there had been almost no contact with him. As far as she knew, he lived in California and had a marginal life. Mother had lived with Stepfather since Beth was eight and they'd married when she was ten. Beth did not like Stepfather, seeing him as bad-tempered and alcoholic. During adolescence, Beth ran away from home twice. She felt going away to college had been the best thing that ever happened. Now, at twenty-four, she was excited about her job, life, and coming marriage. An open-ended question the therapist always asks is, "Looking back on your childhood and adolescence, what was the most negative, confusing, guilt-inducing, or traumatic thing that happened?" For the first time in the session, Beth became tearful and she recounted an incident when she was fifteen in which Stepfather ranted she was a "whore" and he would punish her sexually. He was drinking and hit her, but it was the sexual threat that most scared her. Beth viewed Mother as siding with Stepfather, and was angry at her for not protecting Beth. Beth had been afraid of Stepfather, although there were no sexually abusive incidents. As an adult, Beth was grateful to her parents for their financial and practical support, resumed an amicable relationship with Mother, had a distant relationship with Stepfather, and was committed to having a better marriage than theirs.

Laurie's individual meeting was the first of three emotionally intense sessions. She had a "secret" she'd shared with no one. From the time she was twelve until sixteen there had been a number of sexual incidents involving Stepfather. They occurred late at night when he had been drinking. The activity took place in her bedroom and consisted of rubbing his penis against her thighs or breasts until orgasm. On occasion, there was manual stimulation. There had not been intercourse or attempted intercourse.

Laurie alternated between feeling shame and guilt to feeling anger and revengeful. She was unsure what she wanted to reveal; she didn't want to disrupt Mother's life and marriage. She was angry at Mother for not being aware and intervening on her behalf. Laurie did want the abuse issue aired, and hoped to receive an acknowledgment and apology. Maintaining a close relationship with Beth and Mother was important, but Laurie preferred to remain distant from Stepfather.

The interview with Mother was tense. She was enjoying her life, a successful career in marketing, a vastly improved marriage, and greater freedom and flexibility. The earlier part of her life had been extremely difficult—she'd married her first husband to escape a physically violent, chaotic household. The marriage was horrific. Mother felt her daughters didn't appreciate the courage it took to leave and be a single parent with two young children. The first few years of this marriage were difficult, but her husband had provided a middle-class life, including financing college for his stepchildren. The daughters' adolescence had been very stressful, but all survived and Mother felt it was time to move on with their lives.

Stepfather told how he had come into this struggling three-person family and helped create a solid, financially secure family. He admitted he'd been an alcohol abuser for twenty years and four years ago joined Alcoholics Anonymous. When asked the usual open-ended question, "Almost all stepfathers experience difficulties in parenting. What was the most difficult, traumatic, or embarrassing experience you had as a parent?," he took a deep breath and said, "Did Laurie tell you about our difficulties?" The therapist said, "Yes, but I'd like to hear it from your perspective." At first, Stepfather spoke hesitantly, but then his story of the abuse, followed by guilt, drinking, and more abuse rolled out. He blamed everyone— his wife for not being more attentive, Beth for being an angry, sexually active adolescent, Laurie for being his favorite child, and himself for drinking. He was offered a follow-up session to decide how to deal with the abuse in the family meeting. The day before the individual session, he called and said he'd told his wife and she wanted to attend.

The therapist structured the session so Mother and Stepfather didn't become involved in a self-fulfilling litany of guilt, self-blame, and blaming the spouse. The first question was whether Stepfather was willing to apologize to Laurie and take responsibility for the sexual abuse. The common trap is for the parent(s) to deny or minimize and blame the child (or Adult Child). The guiltier the parent(s) feel, the more likely he/she will act in this manner. Shame and guilt seldom, if ever, promote positive behavior. The therapist said wallowing in guilt and blame would not be in their best interest nor that of their daughters.

One of the hardest things for parents is to assume responsibility for mistakes (including something as serious as incest), apologize, but not negate the value of their lives and family. Mother had the courage to admit a real tragedy had occurred which would be dealt with, not covered up. Males often say if there wasn't intercourse it wasn't sexual abuse. Stepfather, however, was strong enough to admit to the incestuous incidents and assume responsibility for the abuse. Both Mother and Stepfather were committed to their marriage and to repairing the marital bond. They acknowledged that the past had to be dealt with, not ignored or brushed off. Both Laurie (and to a lesser extent Beth) had been victimized and this had to be addressed if the family was to heal.

The family meeting was scheduled as a double session, structured to confront the reality of incest and for Stepfather to apologize. Stepfather began by saying this was the hardest thing he'd ever done in his life. He recounted his motivation for marrying and wanting a cohesive, loving family. He admitted his drinking had been out of control and how frustrated he had felt when things didn't work the way they "should." He had verbally abused Beth because he couldn't deal with her independence and sexuality. He had wanted a better relationship with Laurie, but instead sexually abused her. By this point, all four people were tearful. Stepfather blamed the abuse on drinking and misguided attempts to be a loving father. The therapist pressed him to not equivocate and Stepfather said directly to Laurie that the sexual incidents were wrong and totally his responsibility. She should not blame herself. He apologized for the hurt and trauma.

Beth was startled by the revelation and wanted to go on the attack. The therapist intervened and said Laurie needed a chance to ask questions and understand what had happened.

She'd been carrying the secret too long; she deserved to have a full airing. Laurie's first question was to Mother—"Did you know?" Mother said, "no," but apologized for not being more supportive of Laurie and Beth. Mother couldn't undo the past, but did love and value her daughters and wanted to help them deal with this tragedy.

They agreed to a series of family sessions interspersed with individual and subgroup (couple, Stepfather and Laurie, Mother and daughters) meetings. In addition, each person was given selected self-help readings on dealing with incest. Therapy with incestuous families is difficult, but worthwhile. The focus is dealing with past incidents so each individual and the family system is no longer controlled by secrecy, shame, and guilt. They need to view themselves as survivors, not victims, of incest. Incest does not define the individual nor is it the shameful family secret.

Laurie felt able to proceed with her life, less burdened by the past and secrets, responsible for herself as a person and sexual woman. She felt greater respect for Mother and Stepfather, and closer to Mother. Beth felt more aware of the complex dynamics of families. She planned to use this awareness for the benefit of her future family. Mother had been prone to deny problems. Confronting the past was probably of most value to her. Dealing with these experiences and feelings equipped her to be realistic, yet positive, in her life. She felt accepting and optimistic about herself, her marriage, and adult daughters. Stepfather had been a critical, controlling person. This emotional confrontation opened him in a way he had not experienced. He was not comfortable with the therapist's recommendation to join a psychotherapy group, but did become involved with a church-sponsored spiritual exploration program.

This family and its members benefited by confronting the reality of the past in a therapeutic manner. Beth and Laurie felt aware, deserving, empowered. They were survivors, not victims. Their stories, like those of most therapy clients, are not of instant or perfect cures. There are ambivalent feelings, anger, confusion, and disappointment about the past, as well as problems and issues in the present. The human condition is multi-causal, complex, and variable.

MYTHS AND REALITIES OF HEALING

Does trauma occur? Yes. Do the experiences and feelings need to be confronted and expressed? Yes. Is recovery a process that is in your best interest? Yes. Is it simple and are 12-step programs the only approach? No!

The experiences of childhood comprise a very complex continuum. Some childhoods are loving, nurturing, and relatively stress free and, on the other end of the continuum, some are chronically violent, abusive, and destructive. Within that continuum is a range of childhood experiences, sometimes neglectful, sometimes caring; sometimes dysfunctional, sometimes nurturing; some good parenting, some awful parenting; some loving experiences, some angry experiences. Self-help books and groups tend to view the world of childhood and families as dichotomous, either loving/nurturing or abusive/dysfunctional. These black-and-white labels have value in raising people's awareness that the family of origin was not the happy place it was supposed to be. Groups such as Adult Children of Alcoholics, Violent Families, Incest Families, Adult Children of Dysfunctional Families give voice to the reality of a damaged childhood. Most important, the label unmasks the "secret" and helps the adult realize it was not her responsibility and she need not be burdened by guilt and shame. It gives permission to feel and speak hidden hurts. This is of great value. It is an initial and crucial step in the psychological process of healing. However, it is a cruel hoax to believe it is the most important step and that healing is simply a matter of living out a 12-step recovery program. Expressing pain and nurturing your "inner child" sounds good, but it has led innumerable people down a road leading to the dead end of defining their lives as victims. It is too easy, in this immensely complex and psychologically sensitive area, to fall into simplistic clichés—including our own of "being a survivor, not a victim" and "living in the present, not controlled by trauma of the past."

THE PROCESS OF BEING A RESPONSIBLE ADULT

We wish we could outline a simple three-point or 12-step program, but psychological well-being is a complex process that needs to be individualized. We often recommend 12-step programs, but they are not for everyone. We suggest individual, couple, group, and family therapy, but there are many who do not feel comfortable or benefit from therapy. Some find reading self-help books of value because they learn from people of similar backgrounds, while others find the testimonials and stories simplistic and redundant. Spiritual recovery programs can be of immense help in providing a stable sense of meaning, but many find them abstract, idealistic, and offering little solace. There is not one pattern of abuse and there is no one pattern of healing or method to attain psychological well-being. Ultimately, it is the individual who must weigh the approaches and resources and decide what best meets her needs. The individual must take responsibility for her life and not turn it over to a group, ideology, program, guru, or therapist.

We present information, guidelines, exercises, and suggestions to help you assess and understand your childhood and family of origin. Our emphasis is on the present and future. We confront denial and shame of the past, but warn against putting all your time, energy, and psychological resources into trying to discover or undo the trauma. Understand your childhood in a manner which facilitates acting in your best interest as an adult. The essence of being a survivor is feeling responsible for your life, not feeling controlled by guilt, shame, or trauma. Willingness to deal with difficult issues rather than engaging in avoidance or "if only" thinking is central to psychological well-being. Life is meant to be lived in the present with planning and anticipation of the future, not stuck in secrets or paralyzed by wounds or obsessions from the past.

For most adults, maintaining an emotional connection with their family (or at least some members of it) is advisable. Total rejection of one's family and background is the healthiest coping strategy for some, but they're the exception, not the rule. People are not meant to lead their lives as isolated, alien-

ated islands separate from others. Family is a key element in
most people's emotional support mix. For adults from dysfunctional families, this is difficult. The solution is not a total cutoff
or rejection, but understanding and accepting the limitations,
as well as strengths, of family relationships.

Being a survivor means developing self-esteem. This includes cultivating relationships with personal and couple
friends who value and respect you. A chief function of 12-step
groups is an alternative emotional and social support system.
Most utilize this for six months to two years, while for others
the support group is an alternative family. Support networks
can promote the recovery process and psychological well-being, but there are groups and people that subvert individual
hopes and goals. You can't choose your family; you can and
should choose friends and support groups. When you develop
a clear sense of what you need, you'll begin to recognize which
are the best choices for you.

In one of his most quoted dictums, Freud said, "People
must learn to love and work." The ability to form respectful,
trusting, intimate relationships, and be a competent, successful
person is crucial. Does that mean being married and working
for a large corporation? It could, if that's the right path for
you. But there are many ways to organize a responsible, satisfying life. For example, people have loving friendships, establish a nurturing relationship with an aunt or niece, serve as a
volunteer for a homeless shelter. Competency can mean being
a skilled craftsman, owning a small business, being an involved
childcare person, or a conscientious computer programmer.
Competency means taking pride in who you are and what you
do.

Being a responsible adult includes establishing respectful,
non-abusive relationships, especially with children. One of the
most depressing aspects of the abuse/victim cycle is its potential to be transmitted cross-generationally. People who grew
up in physically abusive families are vulnerable to physically
abusing their spouse and children. This is not predestined,
but is a vulnerability. The responsible adult is aware of his
vulnerability, committed to not falling into that or other psy-

chological traps, and utilizes coping mechanisms and resources to live his life in a respectful manner. For example, the person from a sexually abusive background needs to be aware of and accept the reality of the abuse, be committed to not abuse others or allow himself to be revictimized as an adult and to live his life as a survivor. If he suffers from inhibited sexual desires, he should seek counseling that empowers him to develop sexual self-esteem and facilitates communication about what he needs and values in an intimate relationship.

Above all, being a responsible adult means living in the present with positive anticipation of the future. It means acting in your best interests and having trusting, respectful relationships. Pain and trauma is dealt with, not obsessed about or played out as a continuous repetition in the present.

WHO WE ARE AND THE PLAN OF THIS BOOK

Emily and I are a husband-wife writing team committed to living our lives congruent with the guidelines we present. I have a Ph.D. in psychology and practice individual, marital, family, and sex therapy. In addition, I am a professor of psychology and conduct workshops for professionals and the public. Emily has a degree in speech communication and is a writer and home restorer. This is the sixth book we have coauthored.

We met when Emily was a college senior and I was a second-year graduate student. It was on our third date that we had our first serious talk and first couple agreement—one we have honored through our twenty-six years of marriage. We had both come from families where there was a good deal of anger, violence, and intimidation. Our first agreement was we would not engage in violence or coercion. Honoring that agreement has increased self-respect and respect for our marital bond.

We admit and accept without shame or stigma that we came from families with a moderate to high degree of dysfunction. We have shared this information with our children as they were growing up. We acknowledge the strengths of our parents and the good experiences of our childhoods. Our children had an important relationship with their grandparents, although we tried to ensure there were not violent incidents when they were present. When abusive incidents did occur between grandparents or extended family, we did not hide the reality from our children. We discussed it and encouraged expression of feelings.

We do not view our lives, marriage, or family as anywhere close to perfect. We value our family and take pride and satisfaction in parenting. We hope our children, who are now young adults (twenty-four, twenty-two, and twenty), will look at their childhoods and value the happy experiences, accept and learn from the problems and take responsibility for leading satisfying adult lives. We stay involved in their lives, continuing to care for and about them while allowing them the freedom to create their own lives and relationships.

We wrote this book because theoretically, clinically, and personally we believe adults can lead full, satisfying lives if they accept the complex reality of growing up in abusive, addictive, or dysfunctional families and are committed to being survivors. It would be ideal if everyone's family followed the traditional model of the TV family: the Waltons, or Bill Cosby's modern family, the Huxtables. However, that is not reality. Whether it is the transition of divorce and a blended family, a parent who was depressed or phobic, a family crisis around illness or unemployment, alcoholism, violence, incest, stress, unhappiness, or conflict—most adults had negative experiences growing up.

Our message is positive and hopeful. Abuse and trauma can and should be dealt with, not kept secret or viewed with shame and guilt. Dealing with an abusive childhood does not mean being obsessed by the past nor using it as your defining label. Dealing with childhood pain and trauma means facing complex realities, with the assistance of a therapist, self-help group, books, and, yes, other family members. It means staying away from simplistic "good guy-bad guy" explanations and not falling into the victim role. It means accepting your childhood with its weaknesses as well as its strengths. View your parents as real people, with strengths you'd like to incorporate, and weaknesses which are traps to monitor so you don't repeat the same patterns. In our lives and marriage, the guideline of monitoring vulnerable psychological traps (enlisting the spouse to help in the process) has been effective and worthwhile.

This book is not meant to be read as a textbook. Each chapter is self-contained. We encourage you to focus on chapters and issues which are personally relevant. This book can be read for information and ideas, but it's best used as an interactive learning medium. We encourage you to engage in the relevant exercises and feel free to skip those that would not be helpful. Try the strategies, skills, and coping techniques. Discuss them with your spouse, best friend and, perhaps, siblings or parents.

TO CONFRONT OR NOT

If you choose to confront these issues with your parents and/ or the person who was abusive, keep three guidelines in mind. The first is to identify positive motivation for the confrontation. For example, to gain information and insight into the perpetrator's perceptions about the incidents as well as the historical context for the incidents, and understanding your reactions and behavior at the time. If the motivation is emotional catharsis and blame, we advise you to proceed with caution. The most likely outcome will be defensiveness, denial, counter-blaming, and anger. You risk the danger of feeling revictimized.

The second guideline is to be clear what you want from the parent or abusive person. The usual desire is to have your perceptions validated and receive an apology. This promotes the healing and forgiveness process. Parents who are strong enough to do that are the exception rather than the rule. What is more common is that the parent minimizes the incidents and tries to explain them away. Sometimes the new information and perceptions are helpful, other times confusing, other times negating. If you expect total validation and the parent's guilt to be so great that he will reimburse you (for example, buy you a house) you're in for a rude disappointment. The other extreme is the parent who is offended, makes you feel guilty, and tries to manipulate *you* into an apology. In that case, you need to be assertive and say that's not acceptable, that you are disappointed the parent or person could not meet your request, but that you had a right to raise these issues. Don't allow yourself to be revictimized.

The third guideline is to maintain personal integrity. Confronting a person on incidents from the past is emotionally charged and risky. People's perceptions and feelings are very complex, especially in a difficult and painful area. Only seek a confrontation if you believe it is in your best interest and has a good chance to be successful. If it does backfire, don't allow yourself to fall into the victim role. Remember, the focus is on being a survivor in the present.

We suggest you read relevant chapters and do the exercises in this book before taking any action. Using the guidelines, write down the points on which you want to focus (perhaps in the form of a letter) and share them with a therapist, spouse, friend, or self-help group. Then decide whether to send the letter or have the confrontation. You might decide the benefits are outweighed by the potential emotional costs and backlash. Thinking, talking, and writing promote the healing process.

USE OF THERAPY, SELF-HELP GROUPS, AND OTHER RESOURCES

This is not meant to be a "do-it-yourself" book, used as a substitute for therapy or a self-help group. Our major objection to recovery books is they are overly simplistic and advocate 12-step groups for all problems and people. We believe in the individuality and uniqueness of each person. There are a range of childhood experiences, many forms of abuse and dysfunction, and many ways for a person to address and resolve issues. My clinical work has taught me to respect each person's way of dealing with the past and organizing her life. There is nothing we can say or write that is applicable to every person or circumstance. We believe and care about these guidelines and suggestions, but each person must decide if it is relevant to his or her situation. In clinical work, I make recommendations that are at odds with guidelines presented in this book. I have recommended psychoanalysis, although I believe in reality-based psychotherapy. I have recommended civil and criminal proceedings, although I firmly believe abuse is a therapeutic issue not a legal one (and often litigation results in revictimization). I have recommended totally cutting off contact with all family members, although the usual therapeutic resolution is maintaining family contact while setting realistic expectations. The complexity and uniqueness of each person and family cannot be overstated.

The usual recommendation is a combination of individual and family therapy, self-help groups for up to a year, discussion with trusted others, and reading selected books. Appendix I has specific suggestions about how to choose a competent, qualified therapist as well as assessing self-help groups. Appendix II includes a list of books that are well respected and helpful.

THE CHALLENGE OF BEING
AN ADULT SURVIVOR

Being an adult survivor is a complex challenge. If you are looking for simple answers, you've chosen the wrong book. Being a loving, responsible adult who attains psychological well-being is not an easy task. It is made more difficult by growing up in an abusive or dysfunctional family. You need to devote time and effort to meet this challenge. You have to deal with the past, but even more importantly, deal with what is important in the present. With increased awareness, utilizing all your resources, and a commitment to being a responsible, loving person, it is a challenge you deserve to succeed at. For your sake, and the sake of your intimate partner and children, it is worthwhile to be a survivor. Breaking the pattern of abuse and family dysfunction promotes pride and satisfaction. We hope this book, its guidelines, exercises, case illustrations, and other resources will be of value. Good luck on your journey to healing and psychological well-being.

2
DEFINING YOURSELF AS A VICTIM

When persons or groups are described as victims, the first reaction is to feel empathy and want to help. Stories of neglected or abused babies elicit an outpouring of caring—people volunteer food, clothing, and shelter. Our heart goes out to victims (especially children) and we strive to save them. This helping response applies to victims of natural disasters such as floods or hurricanes. We are a sympathetic and supportive culture. Yet, there is another side to the victim coin—the reaction to victims who are neither children nor overtaken by natural disasters. People victimized by con artists, rapists, economic downturns, ill health, or poor decision making are judged harshly and with disdain. The culture's response is to "blame the victim." This is particularly true if the victim is a man judged to be weak or if it is a woman who has been sexually abused. Our culture values winning and success. People who lose or are abused are blamed and looked down on.

Traditionally, those physically or sexually abused as children, or who grew up in alcoholic or dysfunctional families maintained silence, denying their experiences. In the past decade, however, there has been a dramatic reversal in how adults deal with their abusive childhoods. The Adult Child movement has exploded, encouraging powerful first-person stories (some

by celebrities) of victimization. In books, groups, and on television, people tell they came from an alcoholic family, were
beaten, sexually abused, neglected, humiliated, or observed
domestic violence. Rather than shameful secrets, confronting
abuse has become a badge of honor. The traditional view was
that few children were victimized. The new view is almost all
children are victimized.

TYPES AND INCIDENCE OF ABUSE

The harsh truth is that many children are abused and victimized. We are not the pro-child culture we purport to be. Too
many children are raised in poverty without reliable safety,
shelter, food, and nurturance. Physical and emotional needs of
children are neglected. Rates of family violence, especially
child and spouse abuse, are shockingly high. One in three
female children and one in seven male children are sexually
abused, most by adults they know and should have been able
to trust. Children too often grow up in alcoholic or drug-
abusing families.

By age twenty-five, 95% of people have experienced negative, guilt-inducing, or traumatic incidents. These involve a
range of experiences including the family losing their house,
divorce, having a depressed or phobic parent, a best friend
killed in an accident. Bad things can and do happen to children
and adolescents. Some could have been prevented, while others were inevitable. The most traumatic incidents, however,
involved physical, sexual, and emotional abuse. When perpe-
trated by a trusted person and/or force is involved, the trauma
is even more devastating.

The traditional reaction to an abusive childhood by the child,
parent, and culture was silence. Abuse was unthinkable and
unspeakable and remained secret. Our cultural approach was
to deny or minimize and instead paint a rosy picture of idyllic
childhood.

Our cultural heritage of denying abuse and victimization
needed to be challenged. The pain caused by secrecy and
shame hampered adult functioning and was a major factor in

the continuing, cross-generational pattern of abusive behavior. Abuse and trauma had to be confronted; they could not retreat to the shadows as hidden, shameful secrets.

With child abuse being in the spotlight over the past decade, in a bizarre twist, being an Adult Child is almost "chic."

The claim that everyone is addicted, abused, victimized, or co-dependent negates valid psychological issues and turns the field into a media circus of psychobabble. Make no mistake, we adamantly oppose returning to the days of denial, repression, and minimization. What we advocate is truthfully addressing the complex issues of abuse and, most importantly, focus on the adult as a survivor. The simplistic, black-and-white tales of childhood abuse (vying to be more extreme to obtain media attention) are not a valid way to address these real and powerful issues. It cheapens the psychological pain, downplays resiliency, and negates adult psychological well-being.

Those who advocate 12-step groups as the only approach to childhood trauma are not respectful of individual differences or scientific truth. Focusing on childhood trauma to the exclusion of adult responsibility is harmful to the person and those he is involved with. The pain of childhood trauma must be addressed, but those experiences cannot be relived—there are no time machines. Contrary to the overpromise cliché, it *is* "too late for a happy childhood." Life is lived in the present. A chief guideline is "living well is the best revenge." There are many paths—psychotherapy, 12-step programs, other self-help groups, spouse and close friends, extended family, religious and educational resources—the person can utilize to become a proud survivor.

LESSONS FROM THE HOLOCAUST

The Nazis murdered six million Jews and other ethnic groups in what became one of the most devastating atrocities in world history. It provided a subsequent context to study how survivors of this tragedy coped with their experience and how that affected their immediate families and following

generations. There is voluminous research and clinical literature highlighting individual differences in coping and the outcome.

On one extreme, people were ashamed of being victims of
the Nazis. They hid the tattooed numbers on their arms, viewing it as a symbol of shame. They did not talk about experiences
publicly or share them with their children. They engaged in a
conspiracy of silence. When they had physical or mental health
problems, doctors and therapists colluded in the cover-up by
not asking about the trauma of the Holocaust or exploring if
present symptoms were related to past trauma. On the other
extreme, were those whose entire life and self-esteem were
defined as being a Holocaust victim. They blamed all individual, marital, and family problems on the Holocaust. They
thought of themselves as victims and taught their children the
victim mindset, that the world was unpredictable and scary.
Life was not to be lived in the present, but in fear of the trauma
about to be reenacted.

These extreme reactions have one thing in common: the
person's life and self-esteem are defined by the Holocaust.
The person's self-definition is as a victim—whether a passive,
hidden victim or an angry, public victim. Life was not lived
in the present with planning for the future, but controlled by
trauma of the past. The Holocaust needed to be confronted
publicly as a society as well as on a personal basis. People had
to acknowledge they did survive and teach their children to
think of themselves as survivors, not victims. Research and
clinical evidence demonstrate that those who personally and
publicly confronted the Holocaust experience went on to live
their lives as survivors and raised their children to be survivors
who had healthy families of creation.

This finding is directly applicable to adults raised in abusive,
violent, incestuous, addictive, and otherwise dysfunctional
families. The Adult Child movement has done a disservice by
emphasizing victimization as the self-definition. Adults who
survived childhood trauma can take pride in their resiliency
and lead healthy, loving lives.

Meryl and Don. Meryl and Don had been married five years—four of those spent in 12-step programs. Don was in Cocaine Anonymous, Adult Children of Dysfunctional Families, and Adult Children of Emotional Abuse. Meryl was in Adult Children of Alcoholics, Incest Survivors, and a female co-dependent group. Together they joined Couples in Recovery. In total, they attended fifteen meetings per week. They were so involved in the victim/recovery cycle they had little time for each other or social activities. Meryl was shocked to realize the only friends she had were in 12-step groups.

Meryl's younger sister, Allison, had a baby and asked Meryl to stay with her for two weeks. Allison's life was far from perfect, although Meryl respected Allison's achievements and liked her husband. Meryl and Allison's parents were both dead. Father died of a heart attack three years ago. Mother committed suicide with a combination of pills and alcohol six years before. Allison tried to keep in contact with her brother, although his life was extremely dysfunctional. Both she and Meryl recognized that there was a pattern of family alcoholism. Father and the brother had physically and sexually abused both Meryl and Allison.

Allison dealt with childhood trauma very differently than Meryl. At age eleven, Allison had confided in her best friend and utilized the friend's parents as a surrogate family. A church youth group and minister were a major source of emotional and practical support. The minister had helped Allison get a college scholarship.

Allison did not like Don, partly because of his cocaine use. She'd vowed to marry a man who had no problems with addictive or compulsive behavior. Allison told her future husband the family history of trauma and addiction, not so he would be a shining knight and rescue her, but to be aware of problems, vulnerabilities, and traps. They waited two years before having a baby to assure a strong marital bond. Allison did not share Meryl's need to join 12-step programs, but did not put Meryl down for her approach.

Allison had been in individual and group psychotherapy for

three semesters in college. Therapy strengthened self-esteem and her commitment to a responsible life. Allison realized her family-of-origin problems were real and serious, but preferred to focus her energy on changing the pattern and passing a healthy legacy on to her children. When Allison heard sad or painful family news, she found it upsetting and depressing. She did what she could practically and emotionally, but would not get dragged into repetitive problems. She was not willing to listen to family members badmouth each other and talk endlessly about how they were victimized. Allison was a positive resource, but kept her distance from backstabbing and vindictiveness. She was unwilling to devote energy to fruitless family battles.

Meryl returned home from her stay with Allison with a very different mindset. She was enthusiastic about starting anew with a focus on developing a non-destructive, non-addictive life with less emphasis on past victimization. She was very upset to learn Don had indulged in drinking, smoking pot, and taking pills during the two weeks she was away. Don defensively said he'd not used cocaine and, since he felt Meryl had abandoned him, she didn't have the right to judge him. Don felt vulnerable to neglect and rejection, and several members of his 12-step program agreed Meryl had acted selfishly. Within a week, Meryl fell back in the cycle of guilt and blame with charges of denial, co-dependence, being abusive, and fear of intimacy hurled back and forth. Meryl was urged to attend more meetings and work the program. Don's behavior was described by her groups in a number of ways, from losing his sobriety to acting out fear of intimacy to needing time to heal. Suggestions from the Adult Children of Alcoholics group were contradictory to advice from Incest Survivors.

Don was also getting contradictory advice from his groups. Don had a sponsor in Cocaine Anonymous and a sponsor in Adult Children of Dysfunctional Families who were in conflict. Meryl thought Don got perverse pleasure from playing one against the other. His behavior was very erratic in regard to marriage, drinking and drug use, relationships with family and friends, and financial responsibilities. Meryl was shocked to hear Don had been laid off from work for three months, and humiliated that she was the last to know. When she angrily asked why he'd kept it secret, he hit her and called her a "castrating bitch."

Meryl remembered scenes like this from her childhood. There would be terrible fights, fleeing the house with threats of revenge or leaving forever, and emotional reconciliations which included passionate sex and promises it would never happen again. This was the first time Don had hit Meryl, and she was determined it would be the last. Meryl called their sponsor couple from Couples in Recovery who came over within half an hour (access to ready support for crisis intervention is one of the strengths of 12-step programs). Meryl would not tolerate physical abuse—if there was another incident she would call the police. Meryl said this in a rational, deliberative manner, not hysterical or out of control. Don took her seriously and saw it as real threat to the marriage.

The sponsor couple encouraged Meryl and Don to continue to work in the program and stay in Couples in Recovery. Meryl insisted on the need for professional marriage therapy. Although the sponsor couple supported Meryl's idea, Don balked—he wasn't going to let a professional tell him what to do. Making a decision as part of crisis intervention was not wise. They deferred the therapy discussion to a later time.

As weeks passed, Meryl's trust and respect for Don eroded. No amount of reasoning, pleading, or telling him her feelings would get Don to enter couples therapy. Although he attended 12-step groups on a frequent basis, his behavior continued to be erratic. He blamed problems on being out of work. Meryl was irritated that Don had rejected house painting jobs because he felt they were beneath him.

Meryl entered individual therapy at the community mental health center which offered sliding-fee scale services. Meryl felt she needed to work on self-esteem and marital issues. If Don was unwilling, she would do it herself. She requested a female therapist familiar with 12-step programs and dysfunctional family issues, but who would focus on present feelings and decision making. Meryl was offered a session with a trainee, a middle-aged woman in her second year of social work school. Meryl was assertive in saying her situation was complex and she wanted an experienced therapist. She had to wait an additional three weeks, but felt confident in the clinician she finally engaged.

Meryl found therapy more challenging than 12-step programs, although she missed the informality and emotional catharsis of the groups. Particularly helpful, but difficult, was the therapist's challenge to confront the victim mindset and act in her best interest. Meryl realized she didn't trust Don or her ability to make healthy decisions. The clinician asked Meryl to do exercises involving getting information, writing out problem-solving steps, and developing alternatives and plans. Meryl resisted, saying this was too "Mickey Mouse." In reality, it was painful to realize how deficient she was in these skills.

The most painful awareness involved the marriage. What had attracted Meryl to Don was a combination of romantic idealization with a need to rescue and be rescued. People often marry for the wrong reasons, but nevertheless can build a strong, viable marital bond. However, this was not happening. Meryl saw Don as an immature person who resisted growing up and assuming responsibility. He was minimally interested in developing a healthy marriage, and had no desire for children. Don had enough trouble taking care of himself. Meryl was ready to outgrow the victim role, but Don wallowed in being a victim and used it as an excuse to act out. Don was content to continually blame, feel misunderstood, and live irresponsibly. Meryl wanted more, even if that meant leaving Don.

Meryl and Don had been together almost six years and she was determined to make a good-faith effort to salvage the marriage. Rather than an emotional confrontation with tears and threats, Meryl wrote Don a five-page letter outlining what her feelings were when they first met, insights she gained through therapy and 12-step groups, what she was willing to do, and what she needed from Don to have a satisfying marriage and, eventually, children. She rewrote the letter three times, showing it to her therapist and sponsor to make sure it was positive, clear, and non-blaming.

The evening after reading it, Don was upbeat and initiated lovemaking. Don told Meryl he understood her letter and it was time to throw away the birth control pills and get on with making a baby. Meryl was stunned, both by the miscommunication and the realization she did not respect or trust Don enough to have a child with him. Don wanted a pregnancy as a way of sidestepping personal and marital issues. A baby cannot rescue a marriage, and a child causes further stress.

Don rejected Meryl's reasoning and launched an assault on therapy and her "craziness and selfishness." Meryl would not accept this verbal abuse, but didn't react impulsively. Two days later she approached Don to talk about their lives and marriage. Don said he was tired of talking: she had to accept him as he was. He taunted her about being "confused and a quitter."

Meryl was a victim during childhood, but she was not willing to be a victim as an adult. With the support of Allison, friends, and her 12-step sponsor, Meryl took the hard but necessary step of separating from Don. The next months were difficult and many times she doubted her resolve. When she felt lonely or encountered problems, she wished Don were there, but knew the decision to divorce was rational and healthy. She deserved the life of a survivor, not a victim. This included a respectful, nurturing marriage, not one mired in fighting, acting out, and blaming. She was glad she'd not had a child with Don. Meryl looked forward to the challenge of the future which she hoped would include an intimate, secure marriage and a loving family.

THE SELF-FULFILLING PROPHECY OF VICTIMIZATION

Why do abusive patterns repeat themselves across generations? If you've been victimized as a child, will you abuse your children? Is this predestined? If we believed that, we wouldn't have written this book. You can break the cross-generational pattern of abuse—most people do. It is not a black-and-white issue of being a total victim versus a total survivor. People can and do make significant changes in self-esteem and go on to have healthy families. The goal is to be a better person and parent than your parents. This does not mean being a perfect person or perfect parent. Perfection is an unrealistic goal that will set you up for failure. The goal is to be a better person and a nurturing parent with the hope that your children will be better people and parents. Your goal is to break the cycle of abuse and dysfunction. If you do nothing more than that, you will be successful.

Exercise—Breaking the Cycle of Abuse and Victimization

This exercise involves writing and then discussing with a best friend, spouse, sibling, sponsor, mentor, or therapist. Choose someone you respect and trust and who has your best interest in mind.

On one sheet of paper list the negative, sad, abusive, and traumatic incidents you experienced in your family of origin. Some that have impacted directly on you, others that have indirectly affected you. Be as specific and detailed as possible. Note your age at the time of the incident as well as short-term and long-term effects. For example, at age six Father beat you with a belt on your buttocks and back. These incidents occurred one to three times a week and would last anywhere from a minute to twenty minutes. In the short term, you were frightened, but glad it was your older brother who received even harsher beatings. In the long term, you were angry and plotted to get back at Father, fantasizing beating him up. Anger and angry fantasies played much too powerful a role in your childhood. Try to recall and list *all* abusive or traumatic incidents.

On the second page, list the present ways you act out the victim role. Some are tied directly to childhood abuse. For example, if you had been sexually abused between ages eight and ten by your uncle, with the direct effect that you are aroused by and sexually abuse young boys, you dealt with abuse by becoming an abuser. To change your life and be a survivor you need to confront and change the deviant arousal pattern. An example of an indirect effect of growing up in a neglectful family is to believe children are too demanding. Although you do not neglect your children, neither do you enjoy the role of an involved parent. Another aspect of the victim role is fear of new things and low self-confidence. Be honest and comprehensive in assessing how you play out the victim role in your adult life.

On the third page, list what changes (attitudinally, behaviorally, and emotionally) you need to make to be a survivor. This is not a simple or easy task. List in detail what you need to do to reverse the process of victimization. An example is the angry mother who yells at her children and threatens to beat them (which replicates her experience growing up). She would feel better about herself as a person and parent as well as derive satisfaction from her family if there were less yelling and threats and more nurturing and playful experiences. Another example is the woman who was sexually abused as a child and is frightened her child will be abused. The victimization cycle continues with the frightened parent raising a frightened child. She needs to educate her child about healthy sexuality and sexual abuse and make it clear if there are questions or incidents she is an "askable parent." She would then feel competent as a parent and the child would be aware and confident. What changes do you need to make and what resources are necessary to successfully implement them—help from spouse, a parenting class, a support group, individual or family therapy, close friends?

Look at the list of abusive experiences from the first page. What areas continue to make you feel like a victim? For past incidents which caused guilt or shame, ask yourself whether these reactions have any positive benefits or do they keep you stuck in the victim role. Negative motivation seldom, if ever, promotes positive behavior. What can you do to promote the healing process and think of yourself as a survivor? If you are on the other end of the continuum, angry and obsessed with abuse, you too need to confront the victim role. What is the value of being an angry victim? This also gives the perpetrator and abusive incidents control over your life. As a survivor, you can take back control, live your life in a way that promotes personal satisfaction and is healthy for spouse and children—that is true empowerment. Contrary to the "common-sense" catharsis theory of anger, the more you express anger about the past, the angrier you remain. Develop specific coping techniques that build self-esteem and allow you to feel and behave as a survivor.

Cara—Breaking the Self-Fulfilling Prophecy. Cara was a twenty-six-year-old graduate student who was removed from her family by social services at age six. Father had so badly battered Mother she was hospitalized three weeks. Cara was not physically abused, but there is trauma inherent in observing domestic violence. Although Mother wanted custody, the social worker judged her to be emotionally unstable and unfit. Cara was placed in three different foster homes in the ensuing five years. In one of those homes, an adolescent male sexually abused Cara by coercing her to perform fellatio. Cara told neither the foster parents nor the caseworker because she didn't want additional trouble and didn't feel she'd be believed. Cara wanted Mother back (by this time she had moved to Florida and Cara had no contact with her) or to be adopted, which was unlikely. Although there are long waiting lists to adopt infants, there are few people willing to adopt eleven-year-olds who have been in extended foster care.

Cara was placed in a group foster home until she graduated from high school. The foster parents were strict, emphasized school and church, and were consistent, although minimally loving and nurturing. They were proud of Cara because she did well academically. With the guidance of a caseworker, Cara obtained a college scholarship.

Cara had seen a number of caseworkers throughout childhood and adolescence with little benefit. She wanted to see a "real therapist" and during freshman year saw a psychology intern at the Counseling Center. The intern was used to treating students from relatively stable families and became overly emotionally involved when she learned of Cara's history. Cara felt strongly validated when the clinician cried about her stories of abuse. An Adult Children of Dysfunctional Families group was forming on campus and Cara became a member. Cara saw a different psychology intern whose response to Cara's abusive experiences was similar to that of the first intern—validating but inadequate. Cara excelled academically, but continued to be unhappy. She had few friends outside the Adult Children support group and chose men and relationships which were chaotic and unsatisfying. Cara's weekends involved partying and drugging in an effort to achieve social acceptance and ward off loneliness. These issues were not addressed by the group or therapist; their focus was childhood abuse. Cara shared stories of childhood trauma with friends and acquaintances who were very sympathetic. Cara and friends used her childhood experiences to explain her current unhappiness and self-defeating relationships. Cara saw herself as a victim of the past and used this to explain her increasingly severe personal and interpersonal problems.

When Cara was referred to a new therapist, he was the ninth she had seen. The referral came from Cara's graduate school professor who saw her as a student with great potential, but whose personal problems were interfering with academic progress. The professor was afraid to confront Cara with her irresponsible behavior because it would set off a flood of tears and stories of past and continuing problems. The therapist was respectful and caring, but emphasized the importance of confronting present self-defeating behavior. Cara was resistant, and her 12-step groups questioned whether a male therapist with a reality-based approach was right for her. The therapist, however, made the point that Cara's behavior was leading her into a severe crisis. His phrase, "You need to learn to act in your best interest," was compelling. Cara's self-esteem had been dominated by the victim mentality, rationalizing, and making excuses for present problems.

Since awareness was Cara's forte, this was addressed first. She was confronted with the fact she was violating a prime principle of mental health: "Do not bullshit thyself." In explaining her academic irresponsibility to professors, Cara believed her excuses. As Cara regained academic motivation and competence, she gained the psychological energy to address a problem she had avoided too long—the state of her relationships, especially with men.

Cara hated empty, lonely feelings and sought men indiscriminately to dispell those feelings. The latest fiasco involved a hard-drinking undergraduate who was in danger of flunking even though Cara wrote his papers. Even with Cara present, he'd flirt with other women. Being treated badly was an impetus for Cara to desperately try to please him. She felt compelled to pursue this humiliating and destructive path. She denied the reality of the abusive relationship, instead focusing on her pattern of choosing men similar to those from childhood. Rather than considering this an emotionally useful insight, the therapist labeled it an intellectualized avoidance defense. Cara hated to confront the emotional pain of a breakup and feeling alone. She was more comfortable in an abusive relationship than being her own person. The therapist eventually helped Cara realize leaving an abusive relationship was not an act of abandonment or worthlessness, but a self-affirming choice.

Cara felt accepted and supported in 12-step groups and was grateful for those experiences. She found therapy challenging and hard work. The therapist did not negate learnings from 12-step programs, but challenged Cara to move forward and apply these insights to becoming a survivor. Cara had become complacent in her role as victim.

The personal growth and change process is complex and uneven. Setbacks and poor decisions reflect unhealthy learnings and unresolved guilt or shame. Cara had to confront these blocks and use insights and psychological energy to feel "grown up," competent to lead her life in a healthy, satisfying way. Cara had two guidelines: "You deserve to choose well and act in your best interest," and "Living well is the best revenge."

CLOSING THOUGHTS

A generation ago, victims of abuse or trauma were caught in the conspiracy of silence and denial. Now, it is all too easy to become caught in the trap of defining yourself as a victim. The process of dealing with abuse and trauma is complex, gradual, and needs to be reality-based. She has to confront guilt, shame, and denial. Accept the complex attitudes, experiences, and emotions involved in the abuse and its aftermath. Be aware of the range of feelings from depression to anger, from helplessness to shame. The responsibility for abuse rests with the perpetrator, not the victim/survivor. Rather than blaming herself and feeling guilty, she has to realize she did the best she could and did survive.

Be aware of unhealthy attitudes, behaviors, and emotions which are "excess baggage" from abusive experiences. Confront them. Learn from the past, but don't be controlled by it. You deserve self-esteem and acting and feeling like survivor. Life is meant to be lived in the present with planning for the future, not controlled by abuse and trauma of the past.

3
FAMILY OF ORIGIN:
DYSFUNCTION AND STRENGTHS

Are there any normal, healthy families? Are all families abusive, alcoholic, depressed, neglectful, fearful, angry, divorced, unhappy, or dysfunctional? Or are all families loving, nurturing, cohesive, happy, and functional—except mine? Are 97% of families dysfunctional as the Adult Child movement claims?

The truth is that all families have strengths and weaknesses. The majority of adults grew up in families with difficulties and problems, but strengths and nurturing predominated. They should be grateful for the positive experience, although they too must attend to traps (areas of vulnerability) from childhood. Those from dysfunctional families with abusive childhood experiences will have to work hard and spend time and psychological energy developing self-esteem, healthy relationships, and a successful family of creation. This is not an easy task.

Growing up in a dysfunctional family does not mean you are predestined to have a dysfunctional life and relationships. Theoretically, clinically, and personally we are committed to the concept of being a "survivor" not a "victim." This commitment is crucial for adults from dysfunctional families, whether alcoholic, physically abusive, incestuous, neglectful, mentally ill, or overwhelmed by poverty. People deserve to attain a healthy, successful life. Although it's not fair, adults from dysfunctional backgrounds have to work harder to achieve this because they have more deficits and vulnerabilities and fewer nurturing experiences and resources.

APPROACHES TO FAMILY OF ORIGIN

Just how important is your first family—your family of origin? Very important. Unfortunately, the greater the abuse and trauma, the more impactful. Only recently have negative influences from families been scientifically studied. The traditional emphasis had been family pride, ethnic roots, illustrious ancestors, and honoring your heritage. This emphasis has taken a 180-degree turn as a result of the Adult Child movement, which claims 97% of families are dysfunctional. The adult child, family, and culture had to confront denial—that dysfunctional families are real. Alcoholism, drug addiction, physical abuse, emotional abuse, sexual abuse, incest, eating disorders, gambling, mental illness, adultery, divorce, and abandonment are family dysfunctions that traumatize the child and affect adult functioning.

Between the extremes of awe toward parents and seeing them as evil conveyers of dysfunction is reality. Yes, there are some parents who are saintly and almost perfect, and some who are cruel, evil, and destructive. The vast majority of parents are people with a mix of strengths and weaknesses. Some are stellar parents, attentive and caring, who create cohesive families that nurture individual growth. Other parents create families that are abusive, chaotic, and out of control with little love or caretaking. The majority of families experience both strengths of good parenting and weaknesses of destructive parenting.

Family systems theory examines the family with more sophistication and complexity than the Adult Child movement. Its major contribution is to understand the family as a system where events are related and reciprocal, rather than isolated and simple cause and effect. Family systems theory recognizes that human behavior (especially family relationships) is multicausal and multidimensional. It gets away from the "evil parent-innocent child" or "saintly parent-devilish child" way of describing families. Family relationships are interconnected and complex, with variable and individual affects.

In law and detective work, the focus is finding the "facts," establishing the "truth," judging who is "guilty" and "innocent." The goal is to make reality as clear-cut and black and white as possible. Families, however, don't follow the legal model of evidence or outcome. For relationships, the subjective is as important, if not more important, than objective facts. Feelings, perceptions, and attitudes are crucial. Two people engage in the same interaction and have very different subjective experiences and feelings. This is multiplied when considering emotionally charged behavior such as spanking, drinking, disciplining, or touching. An adult might view the behavior as appropriate or at least within bounds, while the child sees it as abusive or scary. In clinical practice, therapists see adults deny or minimize behavior that on any objective scale would be rated abusive. They also see the other extreme, when an ex-spouse or Adult Child describes behavior as traumatic and causing great psychic pain that most objective observers would view as within the normal range. The reality is that emotional pain caused by abuse and trauma is more a subjective experience than based on objective behavioral ratings. Factors such as motivation, perceptions, feelings, and understanding of intentionality are crucial. In family systems theory and therapy, these factors are crucial in understanding the family and attending to each individual's needs.

To further complicate the already complex family of origin is the effect of memory. What an adult and child remember from twenty years ago is very different. Legal definitions of fact, truth, and guilt are not the appropriate criteria. Psychological studies of memory show it is multidimensional, influenced by a myriad of factors. For example, a man discussed family-of-origin issues with his sister, who is three years younger. They both remembered frightening, intimidating experiences while growing up. However, experiences she remembers vividly could not be recalled or were remembered as unimportant by the man. Experiences and perceptions he felt sure of and had a major influence on his view of the family had little or no impact on his sister. What is objective truth and what is subjective perception? Does it matter that you uncover all incidents of abuse and trauma? Is it even possible?

The family systems approach believes perceptions and feelings need to be understood and communicated because they have most influence on self-esteem. There is a line from a Bob Dylan song, "You're right from your side and I'm right from mine," which reflects what happens in family-of-origin confrontations. Antagonism and a battle of wills often ensues with people angrily going off in their own direction. Some feel like passive victims, some angry victims, some depressed, some enraged. They feel misunderstood and invalidated.

Family system intervention focuses on increasing understanding and communication among family members. The emphasis is on cross-generational patterns of behavior. The parent is understood as a person influenced by a multitude of factors, including his/her family of origin. This gets away from the simplistic "good guy-bad guy" view of families. Family systems theory provides a sophisticated, complex understanding of the multiple causes and multiple impacts of parental behavior and childhood experiences.

RESPONSIBILITY AND BLAME

Who is responsible for abuse and trauma? As a culture, we traditionally "blame the victim." Feeling guilty increases the sense of victimization. Children are *not* to blame for abuse or trauma. Nor are they to blame for parental alcoholism, drug addiction, mental illness, divorce, physical abuse, spouse abuse, and sexual abuse. These are adult problems, and children are not responsible for causing or curing adult problems. Because of their age and role, it is parents, not children, who have responsibility for the family's well-being or dysfunction. Children do not cause families to become dysfunctional.

The issue of responsibility is separate from blame and guilt. Responsibility refers to admitting to a problem, saying you were wrong, apologizing, and committing to not repeating the behavior. Blame is a way of attacking someone or something. Blame is a legalistic concept of judging the person to be the "bad guy," held totally responsible for the negative event and outcome. The person who is blamed is viewed as totally guilty. When people feel guilty about their behavior, this lowers self-esteem and they are more likely to repeat destructive behavior. Guilt feeds the self-destructive cycle; it seldom motivates change. Taking responsibility, expressing sadness and regret, committing to not repeating destructive behavior, and learning a healthier way to relate is the desired goal. Blame and guilt have the opposite effect. It traps people in a cycle of defensiveness, repeating destructive behavior and reinforcing low self-esteem, resulting in shame.

Negative motivation seldom, if ever, promotes positive behavior. Positive motivation, especially concepts of "deserving," "commitment to change," "acting in your best interest," "pride in resiliency," "being a better parent" changes behavior.

Traditionally, adults denied or dissociated the trauma they'd experienced in childhood: keeping "secrets" was a major burden and distorted self-esteem. This caused a multitude of problems, including repeating the pattern of dysfunctional behavior they'd grown up with. Adults from a neglectful and emotionally alienated family had marriages that were unsatisfying and were, in turn, neglectful parents. They experienced a range of psychological problems from alcoholism to sexual dysfunction. The Adult Child movement labeled this trap "blaming self and feeling shame." Blame, guilt, and shame are powerful, destructive motivations.

The Adult Child movement urges confronting denial, admitting you were abused. Twelve-step groups deal with specific forms of victimization such as Adult Children of Alcoholics, Incest Survivors, or the generic Adult Children of Dysfunctional Families. Twelve-step programs present themselves as the only way to deal with the past and achieve recovery. These groups and their writings have done immense good by confronting problems and exposing them to the light of public awareness. They have correctly labeled the problem of child abuse. The child was further victimized by having to guard a shameful secret.

The Adult Child movement made two major mistakes—carrying this awareness to the extreme by encouraging adults to base self-esteem on being victims, and transferring blame, guilt, and shame to parents. Self-esteem should never be identified by a negative. People who say that the most important thing about their lives is that they were victims of incest, children of alcoholics, or abandoned by their family are inadvertently revictimizing themselves. The abuse was real, but by utilizing it as one's primary self-definition, allows childhood trauma to control adult life. Self-esteem is your responsibility and under your control. Don't allow past trauma to define who you are.

Most professionals agree with the concept of defining yourself as a survivor, not a victim. However, there is disagreement over blaming parents and responsibility for family-of-origin dysfunction. When the therapist works clinically with families, she helps them focus on two dimensions—additional information to increase the adult child's understanding, and parental acknowledgment and apology for abusive incidents. The adult child who demands the parent acknowledge, apologize, and offer compensation for any and all abusive incidents is setting herself up for frustration and revictimization. Looking to one's parents for validation is not a proper role for adults. Take responsibility for your life. Utilize information and apology as valuable therapeutic resources. With or without them, you need to validate your experiences so you think and act like a survivor. Does blaming parents and shifting the guilt to them help you? In most cases, the answer is no. Most adults desire to keep contact with some or all family members. Adult relationships are not facilitated by guilt, blame, or shame.

Tom and Lydia. Tom and Lydia were married for four years; they had a one-and-a-half-year-old son and Lydia was four months pregnant. Twenty-eight-year-old Tom came from a divorced family where both Father and Stepfather had been physically abusive. Lydia's family included an older brother who had sexually abused her and parents who were in such conflict over their lives and marriage that they neglected Lydia and her sister.

Tom and Lydia did not discuss family issues when they first met. They strove to impress each other and light a special spark. It was not until they'd been together seven months that Lydia told Tom she was close to her sister (whom he'd met), disowned her brother (who had been in jail and led a marginal life), and was not close to either parent. She asked Tom about his family. He told her that his siblings and stepsiblings had a host of troubles. The only one he felt close to was a brother a year younger. Tom and Lydia did not want to introduce their families to each other until they felt sure of each other.

Tom asked Lydia to move in with him eight months after they'd met. Tom had three brief live-in relationships previously, and Lydia had lived with a man for seven months. She had no desire for another live-in relationship. At twenty-three, she felt ready for the permanent commitment of marriage. She was interested in living with Tom as a genuine trial to see if emotionally, sexually, and practically they could share their lives. Lydia was unwilling to make a commitment unless she believed respect, trust, and intimacy would grow into a strong, viable marriage. Lydia was the initiator of self-disclosure. She did so gradually, to be sure she could trust Tom. Respect and trust have to be earned. Adults from dysfunctional families feel a need to prove something to themselves or their partners and often unwisely enter into relationships that do not deserve the investment. Lydia was aware of this trap. Although she had strong emotional and sexual feelings, she proceeded cautiously rather than being swept away by romantic love. Tom was impressed by Lydia's self-disclosures and seriousness. He was looking for an assertive woman who possessed the strength and purposefulness he had not seen in his mother, sisters, or stepsisters. Tom agreed to live with Lydia as a trial marriage. They wouldn't proceed unless they were sure they could develop a strong, intimate marital bond, quite different from their parental models.

Tom tried to disclose to Lydia his family experiences. When socializing with his brother they traded family stories. Tom took Mother to brunch the Sunday before her birthday and asked Lydia to join them. Two weeks later, Lydia went to lunch alone with her future mother-in-law. Lydia saw her as a nice but sad woman who had made the mistake of trying to live through her children and tolerated two abusive marriages. Lydia, however, respected her for trying and being more nurturing than her own mother. She was committed to having a different life, marriage, and family than either her mother or mother-in-law.

Lydia's observations were helpful in understanding Tom's family of origin and his opening up about abusive experiences. Tom had only discussed the trauma with his brother. He did not want to keep these secret from Lydia, but was unsure what he wanted to share and what she wanted to hear. Was it psychologically healthy to review each incident? Recall each detail? Lydia said the most important thing was not repeating those patterns in their marriage and family. Tom hadn't thought in those terms. Instead of complaining about the abusive childhood and telling "war stories," Tom focused on his feelings about the incidents (both at the time and in retrospect). Seeing Father and Stepfather engage in violence was an example of a male using anger to control his wife and children. Tom had lost contact with Father, who had a marginal life of moving from job to job, in and out of the country. Stepfather mellowed with age and was better with no children at home. With Lydia's encouragement, Tom had a talk with Stepfather. Tom wanted to do it over a cup of coffee, but Stepfather needed a couple of beers to talk. Tom was amazed how differently Stepfather viewed the family—he recalled feeling overwhelmed with financial and disciplinary burdens. He'd never enjoyed being a father; it was a thankless job, but he'd done the best he could. Stepfather loved Tom's mother, but didn't respect her. Tom was determined to establish a very different relationship with Lydia and his own children.

Lydia's parents objected to Lydia and Tom living together. For all their marital and family problems, they were politically and socially conservative. They were against unmarried couples living together and didn't think Tom was good enough for Lydia. Tom was the best educated and most successful person in his family, but that counted for nothing with her parents. This frustrated Tom (as well as reinforced for Lydia how judgmental and narrow-minded her parents were).

Lydia's parents denied the brother's abusive behavior. They pretended and covered up the brother's serious, chronic problems. If they don't think about it, it can't be real. Lydia decided there was no payoff for confronting her parents. She had dealt with the abuse of the past (she'd been in a women's self-help group for fifteen sessions and six months of individual therapy). For Lydia, the important thing was seeing herself as a survivor and leading her life in a way which reinforced self-respect.

With a second child about to be born, Tom and Lydia felt prepared to reexamine the strengths and vulnerabilities of their families of origin. Lydia was pleased her sister and brother-in-law were emotionally close and would be the baby's godparents. Her parents had been financially helpful with a loan for a down payment on their house and gifts of baby furniture. Unfortunately, they continued to be overwhelmed with marital problems and were minimally involved grandparents. Lydia wanted more and decided to have a one-on-one talk with Father. Lydia was saddened to hear Father had decided to leave Mother for another woman. Father tried to get Lydia on his side (as did Mother at a later time), but Lydia made it clear she didn't want to be caught in the midst of their divorce. It was quite a struggle: a heavily contested divorce which extended over five years, where the lawyers came out the only winners. Lydia's question was whether either would be an involved grandparent. She received the answer she feared—their lives and problems came before Lydia and grandchildren, a sad reality. Lydia regretfully accepted this and was committed to being a loving, nurturing parent and, in the distant future, a loving grandmother.

Tom was impressed with how Lydia dealt with her family of origin, accepting the reality parameters without being stuck in bitterness or caught in the hateful divorce. Tom developed renewed respect for his mother, the only grandparent to involve herself with the grandchildren. Being a parent allowed Tom to adopt a mature approach to life, family of origin, and family of creation. He was motivated to be a better person, spouse, and parent. Tom realized good intentions were not enough. He needed to think and read about the father role and, even more important, be active. Lydia and Tom enrolled in a ten-session parenting class sponsored by a community family clinic. Tom realized he would need the support of male and couple friends, and especially Lydia, if they were to have the family they wanted.

Exercise—Strengths and Traps From Your Family of Origin

By age twenty-five, most adults have the maturity and perspective to objectively evaluate parents and family of origin, but it's not an easy task. It is even more difficult when dealing with abusive and dysfunctional families. The focus of this exercise is to objectively and realistically view your parents first as people and then as parents. We suggest writing this and sharing it with spouse, friend, or trusted relative.

Take three pieces of paper and draw a line down the middle of each. On the first page, on the right side, list personal attributes of Mother you liked and respected. Be as specific and objective as possible. Focus first on personal, rather than parental, attributes. Then list positive attributes as a parent. On the left side, list, as specifically as you can, what you view as her personal weaknesses and problems. Then negative attributes as a parent. People tend to be emotional and subjective, whether overly negative or positive. Realize Mother was a person first and parent second. Be specific about weaknesses and idiosyncrasies as well as strengths. The common trap is making generalizations—"she was an angry person," "she was a saint," "she was hateful." Generalizations cheat you of insights and understandings. Focus on specific times, people, and situations. For example, "Mother would become so depressed when Father was drinking she neglected herself and us," "Mother was involved and enjoyed parenting until my older brother was arrested for shoplifting. After that, she was a hysterical tyrant who yelled about every problem." Be clear which characteristics are personal as opposed to which are parental. Some people are more comfortable and competent parenting babies than ten-year-olds; list strengths and problems at different stages of parenting.

On the second paper, use the same format in regard to Father's positive and negative characteristics. Children often think of parents as an inseparable unit. In truth, they are individuals. Give serious thought to what Father was like as a person, separate from his role as parent. Then focus on what you liked and disliked about him as a parent, and review specific times and incidents. Be specific about abusive and negative incidents as well as nurturing and positive experiences.

On the third page, recall significant childhood experiences with your family, both abusive and positive. Focus on specific experiences at different time periods. Be as specific and detailed as possible when listing abusive experiences. Focus on thoughts and feelings both at the time and as you reflect on the incidents. Be aware of situational patterns—who was there, what was said, the behavioral incidents, and consequences. Especially be aware whether you blamed the abuse on yourself, parents, or someone or something else. Did you keep the incidents secret or share them with someone? Did it help, or did sharing make it worse? In retrospect, how powerful were those incidents and how much influence do they have on present self-esteem? How did those incidents influence your view of Mother and/or Father at the time and in retrospect? Do you give those incidents too much or too little power in understanding your family of origin?

Be as specific and detailed as possible when listing positive, nurturing family experiences. What were your thoughts and feelings—both at the time, and as you reflect on your childhood and family? What experiences and learnings contributed to self-esteem and increased confidence in your competencies and achievements? Did you see these as something you deserved and valued, or were they lucky and transitory? Did you have positive experiences with one or both parents, siblings, grandparents, aunts or uncles, cousins, or parent-substitutes? In retrospect, how powerful were these and how much do they influence present self-esteem?

Share these notes and understandings with spouse, best friend, or family members. Their insights and additions can be of value in broadening perspective on your childhood, parents, and family. It is important for self-esteem and family of creation to have a complete, realistic view of your family of origin and childhood experiences.

A PSYCHOLOGICAL APPROACH TO FAMILY OF ORIGIN

Many people find the preceding exercise and approach to the family of origin profoundly unsettling. They wonder what's happened to "family pride" and "family tradition." They're afraid it is so analytical and problem-focused that it cuts out the core of the family. We are sensitive to the concern about the family pendulum swinging from the extreme of the "all loving, all protective family" to the "all dysfunctional, all abusive family." It is no more helpful or true to denigrate and negate the family of origin than to put it on a pedestal.

The goal is to increase awareness and understand family patterns so you are better equipped to deal with your life and family of creation. You will learn more if you approach your family in a respectful manner, with a sense of empathy rather than blaming. We feel strongly about this, although it contrasts with traditional psychodynamic approaches and the Adult Child movement.

The majority of families are not abusive, but the sad truth is that a significant number are. *Every* family has its problems, weaknesses, and areas of dysfunction. Self-respect involves accepting your family of origin in a clearer, more objective manner, aware of strengths and weaknesses. Strive for a functional, loving, and satisfying family of creation, the most important ingredients being self-esteem, an intimate marriage, and parenting as a cooperative team. Family of creation might be the traditional family of a husband, wife, and children, but there are many healthy types of families including blended families, couples without children, single-parent families, and extended families.

Individuals and couples from severely dysfunctional families need to pay special attention to these guidelines. A legacy of a dysfunctional or abusive family of origin requires that time and psychological resources are devoted to establish self-esteem and a successful family of creation. This might not be fair, but it is realistic. You revictimize yourself when you feel helpless and overwhelmed by negative experiences and learnings from your family of origin. Neither self-pity nor blaming parents promotes change. The challenge is to develop increased awareness, resiliency, and commitment to being a survivor. Develop a responsible, satisfying life and loving, healthy relationships—especially within your family of creation.

4
GROWING UP IN AN ALCOHOLIC FAMILY

Alcohol is the most abused drug (legal or illegal) in the United States. Of the 65 million adults who drink, approximately one in seven is alcoholic and another two in seven abuse alcohol on occasion. This affects much more than the drinker. Alcoholism is truly a family disease, affecting the spouse and children. A highly visible result are children born with fetal alcohol syndrome. Their physical and mental development is permanently impaired by the mother's alcohol abuse during pregnancy. Luckily, this is relatively rare. What is much more common, although less visible, is the psychological effects of growing up in an alcoholic or alcohol-abusing family.

Alcoholics Anonymous (AA) realized alcoholism was a family disease and established Al-Anon for spouses and Ala-teen for teenagers whose parents are alcoholic or recovering alcoholics. The largest of the new 12-step programs is Adult Children of Alcoholics (ACOA). This program deals with recognizing that growing up in an alcoholic family has a number of major and subtle effects, both in childhood and adulthood. Some of these involve alcohol—adult children who become alcoholic or who marry alcoholics. Other effects include engaging in compulsive/addictive behaviors such as overeating, gambling, drug abuse, and compulsive sexual behavior. The most pervasive effects involve relationships—friendships, marriage, and parenting. Adults from alcoholic families have a difficult time establishing successful lives and families. Their parental model for healthy adult behavior contains major deficits and distortions.

Contrary to the overgeneralizations of many self-help books, not all adults raised in alcoholic families suffer equally from the experience. Some people saw alcoholism in their families and were motivated to abstain from drinking or drug use. Some families retained a sense of nurturing; symbolic occasions such as birthdays or holidays were observed and families functioned well in spite of the alcoholism. Some escaped relatively unscathed from highly disruptive alcoholic families by establishing supportive, nurturing relationships with grandparents, friends' families, or a neighborhood family.

A majority of adults from alcoholic families, however, experienced significant negative effects. A great advantage of ACOA groups and books is they address issues in a way that reduces stigma. Thoughts and experiences that had been secret are revealed, shared, and validated. It is therapeutic to confront denial, shame, and guilt. Realizing it is normal to suffer aftereffects from growing up in an alcoholic family allows people to validate experiences and strive to lead their lives in a healthy manner.

GROWING UP WITH ALCOHOLISM

A crucial dimension in dealing with adults from alcoholic families is to determine whether alcoholism was acknowledged or denied. Labeling a problem, even if not successfully resolved, is helpful. It is dysfunctional and a severe adult deficit to pretend rather than face reality. Going into the living room and seeing a parent passed out on the couch, no dinner because Mother was too drunk to cook, Father losing his job or driver's license, an out-of-control fight fueled by alcohol, physical, or sexual abuse are experiences in an alcoholic home. The child, realizing the problem is alcohol-related, and the parent or parents acknowledging that reality is helpful. A crucial facet of psychological well-being is ability to perceive and talk about reality rather than engaging in denial or pretending.

An important dimension is whether alcoholism was associated with violence and/or sexual abuse. There are alcoholics who do not act out in negative ways, so-called "happy drunks"—although not as many as claimed. A common drinking pattern is for the alcoholic to become depressed or isolated. He doesn't disrupt the family, but leaves an empty space. Another pattern is the marginally involved parent, who prefers drink to his children. The talkative, distracting alcoholic is another pattern. The same stories are repeated endlessly, and the alcohol-driven conversation takes precedence over children's needs. Alcoholic families experience subtle variations on these themes. For example, Mother may not be too drunk to cook and dinner arrives, but it's over- or under-cooked and some is spilled. It's particularly difficult when children have to pretend everything is perfect. Being able to speak about reality is important for children and adults.

Children take home and parents for granted. They are supposed to remain stable and predictable while the child's world changes—learning in school, mastering a sport or music, growth and body changes, establishing friendships, and increasing independence. Unpredictability characterizes alcoholic households. The more unstable and unpredictable, the greater the dysfunction. Sometimes unpredictable events are major—the parent being arrested or the family having to move because rent money went to drinking. Unpredictability can likewise occur in everyday incidents—a burst of alcohol-driven anger, forgetting to drive a child to soccer practice or not picking the child up after school, an embarrassing incident at a post-season basketball banquet, a parent being drunk at a music recital, a birthday party disrupted by a loud argument. While it's no fun knowing that every Saturday afternoon a parent will be drunk, at least it's predictable and the child works around it. Unpredictable incidents, on the other hand, are disruptive and painful.

A particularly devastating syndrome is the parent being "on

the wagon'' for weeks or months, and then an explosive slip into a binge. The child's anger explodes, with a parental counter-explosion, followed by helplessness and hopelessness. Children, whether five or fifteen, are prone to "magical thinking." This mode of perception is reinforced by TV and movies where there's a clear-cut, happy resolution by the show's end. Alcoholism and the alcoholic family do not fit into this unrealistic pattern, but are complex, multidimensional phenomena not amenable to simple, miraculous resolutions and cures. "Miracle cures," where the person stops drinking and peace and harmony return immediately to the family, rarely occur. Hope and belief in the "miracle cure" impairs the child and sets the stage for unrealistic adult problem solving. When the parent stops drinking, the child and family continue to experience stress and conflict. Alcohol is the major problem, but not the only problem, and sometimes not even the most important problem.

This brings us to the next pattern—the parent stops drinking, but the family does not improve. Stopping alcoholic abuse is necessary, but not sufficient, in changing individuals and the family. Children will recount how they prayed for the parent to stop or vowed to be perfect so the parent would stop. When the parent stops drinking but there remains tension in the house and the child is still unhappy, there is a sense of being duped. The hope everything will be great when drinking stops is unrealistic. Adult child self-help groups believe the myth that drinking is the central, or only, problem. The reality is the lives of children, adults, and families are multicausal and multidimensional.

The last issue is the "gray area" of alcohol abuse. One or both parents view drinking as normal. This is especially prevalent in extended families or ethnic groups where a great deal of interaction revolves around drinking. At a family get-together, the first question is, "What would you like to drink?" It is the norm to sit late into the evening drinking and telling stories. An example is Ireland, where socializing and drinking in the pub are socially accepted family activities. Children view these drinking patterns as normal. Later, during adolescence and young adulthood, they may question whether it was dysfunctional. Did they grow up in an alcoholic family? The parents are defensive and angry at the adult child for questioning their behavior.

Alcoholism and alcohol abuse are not simple, black-white objective judgments. Alcohol problems vary not only in severity, but how they affect individuals and the family at different times and situations. Adult children remember the most frightening, out-of-control, abusive incidents. Parents remember times when drinking was fun and caused no problems. Each is so intent on making her point and having her experience validated, she cannot acknowledge or accept the other's perceptions.

This dilemma is particularly galling for the adult who vividly remembers incidents where the drunk parent chased him around the house threatening to break his neck, the parent driving while intoxicated, witnessing an alcohol-driven fight where the police had to intervene, feeling frightened about the unpredictability of drinking, bringing friends home and being embarrassed to find a parent in a drunken stupor. These memories are very real and painful. The parent saying it only occurred once or three times a year does not suffice to make the memory go away. The parent minimizing or denying the incidents intensifies the adult child's anger and insistence on the overriding importance of the alcoholism. The parent feels attacked, becomes defensive, and counterattacks. The struggle becomes increasingly bitter and self-perpetuating. It generates much heat, but little light.

Parents hate being made to feel guilty and blamed for the adult child's problems. Those who admit to alcoholism often contend there was more to the family and the child's growing up than alcohol abuse. The Adult Child feels invalidated and enraged that her perceptions of abuse and trauma are denied or minimized. She feels as hopeless and out of control as she did when growing up. She feels confused, blamed, and guilty for wanting to discuss alcoholism in the family.

Exercise—Evaluating Childhood and Adult Effects
of Growing Up in an Alcoholic Family

This exercise asks you to do a multidimensional assessment with as much specificity and objectivity as possible. The first part deals with childhood effects of growing up in an alcoholic family, and the second part, the adult effects. We ask you to list not just negative effects, but positives and compensations. Don't minimize or "fake good." Nor should this be a self-indulgent, parent-blaming exercise. It will be most valuable to pinpoint specific pain, abuse, and vulnerabilities and specific strengths and compensations. You could do this exercise alone or with siblings, close friends, or spouse.

Use a chronological format to organize alcohol-related incidents. How old were you when you became aware a parent (or parents) had a drinking problem? How old when you observed a negative drinking incident? How old when you became involved in a drinking incident?

Did one parent or both drink? Were other family members involved in problem drinking (grandparents, uncles, aunts, in-laws, older siblings, cousins)? How old were you when you first asked a question about drinking? Did you receive an honest answer or were you told a lie?

It's unusual for drinking patterns to remain constant. The most common pattern is that over time alcoholic behavior becomes more extreme, but is interspersed with periods of relative calm. Was the drinking worse when you were a pre-schooler, a child, during adolescence, after you left home? Were you blamed for parent's drinking (e.g., "If you were a better child, I wouldn't drink so much")? Did you try to make the parent stop, pray the parent would stop, or threaten that if the parent drank you wouldn't talk with him or would run away from home?

Did you talk to anyone about alcoholism or was it a "shameful secret?" What was the most frightening, negative, or traumatic incident you observed? What were you thinking, what did you do, how did you feel? Did incidents cause nightmares or flashbacks? In retrospect, what do you think and feel about that incident? How impactful was it?

As an adolescent, what were your attitudes and values regarding drinking? How old were you when you had your first drink? What was it like being drunk for the first time—what did you do and how did you feel? Did you use and/or abuse other drugs? What did your parents say and do about your alcohol and drug use? In retrospect, what do you think of your adolescent alcohol and drug use?

What were the strengths and compensations of growing up in an alcoholic or alcohol-abusing family? Can you identify direct effects (for example, learning to be independent, problem solving, and using community resources, developing a close relationship with an uncle or neighbor who was a father substitute)? Were there indirect effects (being sensitized to the pain and hurt of others, developing close relationships with siblings or friends, becoming involved with religious or community youth groups)? Those who claim there's an advantage of growing up in an alcoholic family because it builds character and teaches you to deal with adversity are, in our opinion, engaging in wishful thinking. People take pride in learning and surviving, but the idea you should be grateful for the challenge of growing up in an alcoholic family is nonsense.

An oft-cited advantage, however, is awareness of the trap of alcoholism and commitment to moderate drinking or abstinence. A compensation is gaining the strength to survive adversity (the analogy of going through family boot camp), which increases self-confidence. People serving as a substitute family or mentor make the child aware others can be trusted and depended on. Learning that people are responsible *and* responsive is important. A negative legacy is the feeling of isolation and being trapped in an abusive, secretive family.

If the parent comes to grips with alcoholism and overcomes the problem, it is an inspiring lesson about the ability to change and grow. Conversely, a parent being rehospitalized or rearrested can be a powerful negative lesson, instilling attitudes of helplessness and hopelessness.

Adaptability is another important compensation. Children from alcoholic families often experience multiple house and school moves. Divorce and remarriage are quite common. This challenges the child to adapt to new living and interpersonal situations. In our mobile, changing society that can be an important life skill. Growing up in an alcoholic family challenges the "fairy-tale world of childhood," which is not a bad thing.

After you've reviewed learnings from childhood, focus on adult functioning. What are the problems or traps in your present life? For example, a coping mechanism many children use when dealing with a physically or emotionally abusive incident is dissociation. They turn off feelings associated with out-of-control drinking. Dissociation is a means to pretend something isn't real, shutting out negative incidents and feelings. This can be useful to defend against childhood trauma but is maladaptive in adulthood. Adults need to be aware and responsible, not dissociated. Many coping mechanisms that help in childhood are self-defeating in adulthood.

Examples of traps for people who grew up in alcoholic families include abusing alcohol or drugs, choosing inappropriate friends or intimate partners, not being assertive (instead passive or aggressive), being anxious or depressed, poor problem-solving skills, not managing job or money, sexual dysfunction, eating disorders, poor parenting skills, difficulty in maintaining relationships—in other words, a whole range of attitudinal, behavioral, and emotional problems. Can all these be blamed on growing up in an alcoholic family? Remember, human behavior is multicausal and multidimensional. Be frank and honest with yourself (and others) about adult problems. Don't blame everything on childhood or parents.

Most important, use awareness and insights in a productive manner. Differentiate alcohol-related problems from others. The crucial factor is taking responsibility for your life and changing problem behavior. Recognizing the problem is a necessary first step. However, saying "these are Adult Child traps" is self-defeating. Awareness of childhood roots are helpful only if they serve to motivate the adult to address the problem. Too many children of alcoholics take a blaming, self-pitying stance rather than assume adult responsibility and successfully deal with problems.

List adult problems in one column. In the second column, estimate what percent of the problems came from growing up in an alcoholic family. In the third column, outline your plan for changing the problem behavior. Remember, "Living well is the best revenge." Build self-esteem, quality relationships, competencies, and a family of creation which are healthy and satisfying.

MULTIPROBLEM FAMILIES

Seldom is alcoholism the only family problem. Family problems are cross-generational, involving job and poverty issues, depression and hopelessness, poor parenting skills, unsuccessful blended families, abuse of drugs, compulsive behavior (gambling, eating, or sex), neglect or physical abuse, spouse or sexual abuse, bankruptcy and multiple family moves, learning disabilities, academic or behavior problems, and problems with law and/or social services. Often multiproblem families have (at one time or another) had a court social worker, a probation officer for the adult and a probation officer for the adolescent, a public health nurse and a school nurse, a protective service worker and a school social worker, and as many as four different lawyers. With these overlapping domains and interventions, the family feels no one understands them or is working in their best interest—and often they are right.

Mental health workers often feel overwhelmed dealing with multiproblem dysfunctional families, especially when problems are chronic and cross-generational. If professionals feel overwhelmed, what about the child growing up in such a family? Or the adult who has come from this family? Growing up in an alcoholic, multiproblem family is painful and makes the person vulnerable to a number of destructive traps.

Awareness is vital. The person needs to devote time, psychological energy, and professional resources to overcome these patterns. Coping strategies and techniques can be of great help. Rather than striving to overcompensate and have a "perfect" life, he needs to commit to living a more functional life. Instead of being driven by shame, guilt, and proving something, he deserves to succeed and be committed to a non-alcoholic life. When bad things happen and there are setbacks, rather than giving up and getting farther off track, he takes a problem-solving approach with the goal of regaining equilibrium. Carefully monitor traps evolving from the family of origin. Develop relationships with trustworthy people who promote living a responsible, respectful life. Recognize there were strengths in growing up; don't be controlled by the "victim" mentality. Have clear, concrete personal, marital, and family goals. Maintain contact with non-alcoholic people from the family of origin, and don't get sucked into destructive fights and patterns. Life is meant to be lived in the present with planning for the future, not controlled by the alcoholism and trauma of the past.

Vivian and Edward. It's not unusual, although not recommended, that children of alcoholics marry each other. Vivian left home at eighteen for a job, and was a twenty-three-year-old part-time community college student when she married Edward. She had established a career as a medical secretary. Edward was also twenty-three, left home at seventeen, spent four years in the Air Force where he got a GED and training as an electronics technician. They met at a club and their dating focused on dancing and friends. It was not until they decided to marry, exactly six months after they met, that they were introduced to each other's families. Vivian and Edward were trying to impress the prospective spouse and were afraid their family would make a poor impression. They engaged in a mutual cover-up.

In Vivian's family, both parents as well as aunts and uncles were heavy drinkers. Mother's pattern was clearly alcoholic, which Vivian believed was a cause of her premature death at fifty-two (five years after Vivian's marriage). Mother would drink consistently, but the disturbing pattern was going on four- or five-day binges. Vivian was the youngest of three; she had a sister eight years older and a brother five years older. Mother's binges were frightening because the family's world was turned upside down. Vivian turned to her siblings for support, but they were busy with friends. Vivian was most impacted by Mother's alcoholism.

Father was a consistent, heavy drinker but, with two exceptions, always seemed in control. However, those two incidents were seared in Vivian's memory. One involved drunk driving—Father would not stop even though Mother yelled at him, while eight-year-old Vivian cowered in the back seat. Father reacted by driving faster and more erratically, until stopped by a police officer. The second incident was a physical confrontation between Father and the eighteen-year-old sister. Father was rageful and hit her so hard he drew blood. Vivian remembers thinking she would leave home peacefully rather than subject herself to that kind of abuse. Increasingly, Vivian built a life independent of her family. She reacted to her parents' drinking by being almost a teetotaler.

Edward's family was alcoholic, but very different from Vivian's. Edward viewed Mother as a saint, a passive victim of Father's alcoholism. Father was a skilled construction worker who often worked away from home or was laid off; but whether at home or away, he maintained an uninvolved, distant stance. Once a month there would be a massive eruption of anger and chaos, associated with out-of-control drinking. Edward and his four siblings were terrified and angry. They felt guilty Mother took the full brunt of the abuse.

Edward didn't verbalize it, but he subconsciously believed families functioned better when fathers weren't around—an attitude that caused great problems in his family of creation. Edward reacted to his Father's alcoholism by seeing the problem as Father being a "mean drunk." Edward began drinking with friends at sixteen, and saw himself as a fun, social drinker. Because his drinking pattern was so different from Father's, he never envisioned it would be a problem. Edward dissociated himself from Father, saw himself as a good guy, and Mother's favorite child. In the service, hard drinking was the norm. Edward prided himself in staying away from the arguments and fights so many servicemen get into. Edward believed he carried no negative legacies from his family of origin.

Both Edward and Vivian were shaken when they met each

other's families, but because they didn't want to hurt the future
spouse's feelings or raise hard issues about their impending
marriage, they didn't share reactions. Vivian liked Edward's
mother, but didn't want to be the martyr her future mother-in-
law was. Vivian found her future father-in-law's emotional
distance and passivity foreboding. Edward was shocked at the
amount of alcohol Vivian's family consumed, and was totally
turned off by her mother. There was an unspoken competition
as to whose family was sicker.

Vivian and Edward were wary and cynical toward doctors
and mental health professionals. Their parents had been dis-
trustful of attempts by physicians, AA, and alcoholism counselors to change drinking patterns. Vivian thought physicians
colluded with her parents to rationalize and deny problems.

Seeking individual or couple therapy was not an option, so
it took a major crisis to propel them into a therapist's office.
The crisis was that after four years of marriage, Vivian learned
Edward was having affairs. By then they had a sixteen-month-
old son and Vivian was six months pregnant. Edward minimized the affairs, saying it was with women he met at a bar.
Edward labeled them (correctly from his point of view) as high-
opportunity/low-involvement affairs. Vivian reacted angrily
because he'd broken their marital trust bond. Vivian was dedi-
cated to establishing a stable life and family and saw Edward
as the enemy who was destroying her dream. Edward claimed
she was overreacting and was "crazy" like her mother. This
pushed a "hot button" (hitting below the belt) and Vivian told
Edward to leave. When they presented themselves for therapy,
they'd been separated two weeks and saw therapy as a last-
ditch effort to save the marriage.

Each felt victimized by the spouse. One legacy of growing
up in an alcoholic family is lack of trust in intimate relationships, and feeling issues do not get successfully resolved.
There is a tendency to react impulsively and emotionally. The
therapist emphasized "acting in your best interest" and "making agreements that enhance self-esteem and the marital
bond." These attitudes and skills are deficient in adults from
dysfunctional families, and were clearly lacking with Vivian

and Edward. The focused problem-solving structure of therapy was of great benefit, both in dealing with the immediate crisis and learning skills to inoculate against future crises.

The therapy format was seeing them together first, then an individual session to review psychological and family history, and a couple feedback session to propose a course of treatment. Although the marital bond of respect, trust, and intimacy was frayed, it was still intact and both desired to rebuild the marriage. The longer a couple remain separated, the harder it is to resume the marriage because frustration, suspicion, and anger build. Living under the same roof facilitates revitalizing the marital bond.

The first focus was on reaching agreements about drinking and affairs. As a crucial step in rebuilding trust, Edward agreed to drink only in a social context with friends and stay away from the bar scene. Further, he would be involved with the pregnancy, including attending childbirth classes and being present for the birth. They renewed their commitment to marital fidelity and resumed their sexual relationship. Vivian agreed to not play the "guilt, retribution, punishment" game she had seen so often in her family.

Once the marriage stabilized, individual and couple sessions explored effects of growing up in an alcoholic family and identified specific traps. The trap they shared was to pretend nothing was wrong and use wishful thinking as the favorite coping mechanism. They learned problem identification skills and practiced problem-solving exercises between sessions. Utilizing these skills increased personal and marital confidence. Drinking and affairs were Edward's way to avoid dealing with issues. Vivian's vulnerabilities were low self-esteem, fear life would go out of control, and lack of confidence that family problems could be resolved. For Edward the traps were to downplay problems and be minimally involved in parenting and family issues, believing that was Vivian's role. A sign of an intimate marriage is sharing vulnerabilities and trusting the spouse to respect the disclosure and be supportive instead of using it as ammunition in a fight.

Vivian and Edward wanted a healthier marriage and family

than their families of origin. They became aware of the hard work needed to achieve a viable marriage and family. Couple therapy was only one step. They established personal, couple, and family goals and used community and church resources to help keep their lives on track. Vivian attended eight months of Adult Children of Alcoholics meetings and did a good deal of reading. Edward attended six meetings, didn't find them helpful, and felt the reading to be "pop psychology" and unhelpful. They agreed to join a six-month class for couples with young children. They returned for periodic six-month therapy check-ins for two years. If things got off track, they would recognize it quickly and reenter therapy.

COPING WITH DEFICITS CAUSED BY GROWING UP IN AN ALCOHOLIC FAMILY

Are problems adults experience caused by alcoholism, by family dysfunction resulting from alcoholism, or traumatic, painful incidents involving alcohol abuse? Or are problems caused by not having a positive model of adult and family functioning with deficits in attitudes, skills, and emotional awareness? The answer varies, depending on the person's childhood and adult experiences.

The Adult Child approach emphasizes the role of alcohol and dysfunctional family experiences. Recent research and intervention programs emphasize poor modeling and skill deficits. This is an optimistic way to approach adult problems. You can learn attitudes, skills, and emotional expression which builds self-esteem, a successful marriage, and family of creation. That's a realistic, positive approach, but not simple or easy. The greater the deficits, the more important that people from alcoholic families devote consistent time and psychological energy to reaching goals and keeping life on track. For chronic, severe problems, there is a need to use additional resources whether individual or couple therapy, friends or extended family, a self-help group, community or religious resources, or psychoeducational courses.

People from severe alcoholic or dysfunctional families complain about the bad hand they've been dealt and the struggle required to avoid personal, alcohol, relational, or parenting traps. A typical complaint is that their families drag them down, and they have to rescue parents (or siblings) when they themselves need support. They compare themselves to friends who have family support—both practical and emotional. Where alcoholism remains rampant in the family of origin, the hard reality is that you will get little support and will be asked to intervene in crisis situations with parents and siblings.

We suggest the following guidelines. The first priority is personal integrity and self-esteem. It will not help anyone if you allow your life to become unmanageable and out of control. Your marriage and family of creation should take a higher priority than family of origin. You are more likely to influence and succeed with your spouse and children. It is impossible for adult children to cure their parents; you're lucky if you can make minimal changes. Parenting one's parents is very difficult.

It is crucial to keep clear, realistic boundaries between the problems of others and your life. Don't make their problems yours. It is important to recognize the difference between alcohol-driven behavior and the person. It is healthier to be angry at the alcoholism, rather than at the person. Last, but certainly not least, realize you cannot undo the past or receive compensation. Life is meant to be lived in the present with planning for the future, not controlled by guilt, anger, or alcohol abuse.

5
SPOUSE AND CHILD ABUSE

One of the supposed advantages of growing up in American society is feeling safe and secure. America is touted as a middle-class society, offering safety, security, a home, access to quality health care, good education, and the opportunity for wealth and happiness. Violence related to crime and drug activity receives a great deal of media attention. The unfortunate reality is, however, that the home is the major source of violence in our supposedly middle-class society. Physical abuse of spouse and children occurs with alarming frequency. If you add neglect and emotional abuse, it is clear the problem of domestic abuse is prevalent.

Why does domestic violence occur? Like any complex phenomenon, it is multicausal. A prime factor of domestic violence is that it is shrouded in silence, secrecy, and shame. Violence is a learned behavior and modeling is a very powerful learning medium. People who engage in domestic violence are likely to come from families where they saw spouse abuse or were physically abused as children. Although abuse occurs among all religious, socioeconomic, ethnic, and racial groups, it is most prevalent in groups that tolerate, or at least don't condemn, domestic violence. Groups that emphasize male superiority or accept violence as a means of expressing anger have high levels of spouse and child abuse. When a person grows up in an abusive family, violence is mistakenly viewed as "natural." Spouse and child abuse needs to be confronted as unacceptable.

PATTERNS OF ABUSE

Is domestic violence a black-and-white issue? Yes. Spouse and child abuse is never okay. Almost everyone is opposed to spouse battering or child battering, but less violent forms of abuse are tolerated. Although difficult to establish reliable data, the best estimate is that 15% of couples experience at least one incident of battering, defined by use of weapons or sufficient force to cause bruises, blood, or a broken limb. Spouse abuse, defined as hitting or beating used to dominate and control the spouse, occurs at least once in approximately 50% of marriages and is a chronic problem for 10–20% of couples. Child battering, defined as use of physical violence involving a weapon, bruising, blood, or broken limb, is estimated to occur with 10% of children under twelve and 15–20% of adolescents. As many as half of those children experience severe, chronic abuse. With growing public awareness, child battering and severe abuse is condemned, but less physical forms of child abuse continue to be tolerated.

Spouse and child abuse occurs in 50–60% of families, at least on an occasional basis. The most common pattern is spontaneous, anger-driven intermittent incidents. Under conditions of stress and frustration, the verbal argument accelerates to spitting, pushing, hitting, and/or throwing. With children, arguing turns into spanking, which accelerates to hitting and beating with a belt. This can occur twice a month, every three months, or once a year. Although infrequent, it makes for a stressful, unpredictable environment to grow up in. The sense of family peace and security has been broken and is not easily repaired.

Another issue is emotional abuse and neglect, which causes major psychological damage. Neglect says the child and his needs don't matter; he doesn't deserve to be attended to or nurtured. He is insignificant and unworthy. Emotional abuse takes many forms, but the common thread is that it causes low self-esteem. The child or adolescent meets a constant barrage of negative feedback—he's dumb, ugly, not as good as the child next door. Under these circumstances, he would prefer neglect to emotional abuse. He feels hateful toward himself; no matter how hard he tries, it's never enough. The child is told he should be grateful for having a roof over his head, food and clothes, and to stop whining and complaining.

Neglect has to be severe to require social service intervention. It almost requires abandonment, e.g., there is no parent at home for two or more days, the child is unable to get into the house, there is no food in the home, the child is allowed to skip school for days on end. Unless there is evidence of physical abuse, it is difficult to intervene in cases of emotional abuse or neglect.

The final issue is very controversial. It is the so-called "gray area" of abuse. With children it involves ten spanks instead of three, for teenagers it's pushing and shoving and being "grounded" for two months, for the spouse it's being slapped and intimidated into silence. Most people would say that's inappropriate, but would not label it abusive. Many believe any spanking is wrong, but the majority feel one to three spanks on the buttocks is acceptable. Most people would consider "grounding" a teenager an appropriate mode of discipline, but that a two-month "grounding" is extreme. Many object to any physical hitting between spouses, but some tolerate throwing things, slapping, or shoving with an open hand.

Of course, there are gradations of domestic violence. Those who maintain there is no difference between battering and spanking do not help the cause of spouse and child abuse. Our belief is the home should be a non-violent environment. Both the man and woman need to be committed to resolving issues by talking and agreements, not physical intimidation. This includes not pushing, slapping, hitting, spitting, or kicking. A sense of physical security is the bedrock of marriage and family. In parenting children (especially over the age of six or seven), spanking or other means of physical punishment is unnecessary and accentuates problems. There's no doubt physical punishment with adolescents sets up a destructive family environment. If physical punishment is to be used with young children, it needs to be limited to three spanks on the buttocks with clothes on. Physical punishment which exceeds that is likely to be acting out the frustration and anger of the parent, not for the "good of the child."

RELATIONSHIP BETWEEN SPOUSE AND CHILD ABUSE

Spouse abuse and child abuse are separate phenomena, but often interrelated. Some families suffer spouse abuse, but the children are well treated. There are families where children are abused, but parents treat each other respectfully. The most common pattern is one in which spouse and child abuse occur together, both spouses fight and both abuse the children. If it's all right to hit your partner, why shouldn't it be all right to hit your child? Some couples take frustration and anger out on each other, but have an implicit (or even explicit) understanding that it is not acceptable to hit children. In some families, use of physical force is restricted to males. In other families, the husband will hit the wife and male children (but not female children). Males are more likely to be physically abused, while females are more likely to be sexually abused. Child abuse is more frequent in single-parent and blended families. It is more common among adults who grew up in families where there was violence. The pattern of family violence is cross-generational. The commitment to not repeat this destructive pattern is crucial. To have a non-abusive family of creation, the person has to develop healthy attitudes, skills, and emotional responses.

Exercise—Assessing and Understanding Spouse and Child Abuse

This exercise is best done with others whom you respect and trust—siblings, best friends, spouse. The motivation is not guilt or blaming, but to assess and understand experiences with physical abuse so the pattern will not be repeated in your life and family of creation. The format is to review physical abuse experiences as a child and then examine traps as an adult. Your motivation is to live life as a survivor, not as a victim who revictimizes himself and his children.

We suggest focusing first on spouse abuse, and reviewing incidents chronologically. When was the first physical incident between your parents that you heard about or witnessed? (People find it easiest to recall the most violent incident.) Studies of spouse abuse indicate there is a building pattern, not a single incident. There is a period of tension and alienation, accompanying verbal clashes, name-calling, and threats. Clashes accelerate in frequency and intensity, including throwing, spitting, pushing. Some couples experience a single incident, but for most it is a series of incidents building to a crescendo. Violence increases in intensity and dangerousness from a single punch to a series of punches, from threatening with a knife to cutting with a knife, from a bruise on the arm to a broken arm.

Were spouse abuse incidents one-way or did both engage in hitting? Was it done in front of children or others, or always behind closed doors? Was it circumscribed to a half hour, or did it extend over days or weeks? What were the most violent and scary incidents? Was alcohol involved? Over 50% of spouse abuse occurs while one or both spouses are drinking. Drinking is not an excuse for spouse or child abuse, but when drunk, the person's controls are lowered, resulting in violence or abuse.

Did the pattern of spouse abuse increase, decrease, or remain the same as you grew up? Did your attitudes change? Did you blame Father, Mother, yourself? Did you try to stop the abuse or realize it was an adult problem? Did you talk to anyone about this or was spouse abuse a shameful family secret?

Now to the more personal and painful topic—child abuse. Review this chronologically and as specifically as possible. The tendency is to be overly subjective and emphasize only the most severe incidents.

What was it like before age five? Were your parents nurturing or neglectful? Was the mode of punishment scolding, time-out, spanking, hitting, beating with a belt, or more violent means? From six to twelve, what was the pattern of punishment? If abusive, what exactly happened? Did it involve both parents? Was it a consistent or intermittent pattern? How frequently did it occur? For many children, abuse is chronic and severe. For example, each time Father got drunk and/or angry, he would beat the oldest child with a stick while the other children had to be present to witness it. Children said fear of what could happen if the violence got out of control was the worst thing; others recall the physical pain, fear as they were driven to the emergency room; and still others remember that being humiliated and called names was worse than being hit. Although the person involved is usually a father or stepfather, others report brothers, grandfathers, uncles, or stepbrothers being the perpetrators. Children, especially boys, feel particularly angry if they are physically abused by a female relative—whether mother, grandmother, stepmother, older sister, stepsister. It is a reversal of the cultural stereotype: women are not supposed to be aggressive, and certainly not abusive, especially with a husband or son. The truth is that some women are abusive. Usually they were physically abused as children. Don't deny or minimize. List all abusive incidents, as well as thoughts and emotions at the time of the incidents and subsequently.

What negative learnings occurred as a result of spouse and child abuse and how do they affect you now? Be aware of present thoughts, feelings, and behavior as a result of observing spouse abuse or being physically abused as a child (including observing abuse of siblings). Every person has learned patterns of behavior as a function of growing up. It is necessary to have a strong commitment to not repeat the negative patterns in your life and family of creation. How prone are you to be angry and abusive? In what ways do you continue to feel victimized by spouse or child abuse? The more you feel like a victim, the more these learned patterns of abuse will dominate your life. If there has been spouse or child abuse in your adult life—whether by you, you've been abused by your spouse, or your spouse has abused your children, we strongly urge you to seek professional therapy. You can be the last generation that experiences spouse or child abuse. This is not a legacy you want to convey to your children.

A PERSONAL NOTE

As we discussed in the Introduction, not long after Emily and I began to date, we disclosed that we both came from families in which there was anger, intimidation, and spouse abuse. In Emily's family, both Mother and Father engaged in hitting and pushing. In my family, it was one-way: Father ruled by threats and intimidation. When he lost control, he could be quite frightening. Emily's parents were not physically violent with her, but my father was with me, although not with my sister.

Emily and I were committed to not repeating the pattern of violence in our lives and marriage. We agreed that to be viable and worthwhile, marriage needed at its base a sense of trust which would be broken if there were violence. We have been married twenty-six years and are proud we have honored our agreement.

We were equally committed to having no incidents of child abuse. We wanted to be both nurturing and disciplining for our children, but not violent or abusive. For me, it was a difficult struggle to not lose control when disciplining the children. I wanted to be an involved father, although I was a less skilled and confident parent, especially with young children, than Emily. She loved parenting babies and young children, although had a more difficult time with adolescents. Our parenting was not perfect (as our three children will readily attest), but there was no violence or abuse. We helped and supported each other through difficult parenting times. We enjoyed parenting, and hope our children will not be in danger of spouse or child abuse in their families.

ACCEPTING THE REALITY OF CHRONIC, SEVERE CHILD ABUSE

What about those who grew up in families where there was chronic, severe child abuse? How can they accept that reality? How do you deal with that pain and feel like a survivor?

Whether through therapy, self-help groups, religious healing rituals, or being a social activist speaking against spouse and child abuse, it is crucial to confront the issue of violence in your family of origin. Accepting and dealing with a violent, horrendous past is not easy, but what choice do you have? You cannot change the past. The challenge is to not be controlled by trauma and not repeat the pattern in your life and family of creation. Even if family violence was present for three or four generations, you owe it to yourself to be the person who breaks the cycle. You and your children deserve to live in a non-abusive environment.

Many people feel a need to compensate for pain by providing the perfect nurturing family. When people set unrealistic, perfectionistic goals, they not only fail but make themselves vulnerable to falling into abusive traps. People from chronic, severely abusive backgrounds need to give themselves permission to utilize all available resources: friends and family, self-help groups, and professional therapy, to keep their life on a non-violent, non-abusive track. Maintain realistic expectations for yourself, marriage, and parenting. At a minimum, you want to function better than your family of origin and give your children the gift of growing up in a non-violent family. Don't try to be perfect, but to be non-abusive. You'll have a healthier, more nurturing family if you enjoy the process rather than feeling burdened by perfectionism. With the pressure removed to compensate for the pain of the past, it's easier to be a "good enough" parent.

Victor and Maria. It's not unusual for people from physically abusive backgrounds to meet and marry. Often, marriage is the means to escape a violent, chaotic home environment. These couples need to work especially hard at developing a non-violent marriage. View this as a challenge, not a burden. That is the approach Maria took, but Victor resented having to work so hard at life and family.

Maria used family problems as an excuse for poor academic performance in junior high. She remembers two guidance counselors: the one in seventh grade who talked to her about being victimized by family violence and made Maria feel bad about herself because she came from a violent family. Maria's tenth-grade counselor took a different approach. She encouraged Maria to be resilient and rise above family problems. The counselor encouraged Maria to join the marching band and improve grades so she was eligible for the honor society. The counselor told Maria she couldn't change the fighting between her parents; but that when things got bad, to use her grandparents and aunt as resources. Maria focused on strengths and new competencies, and found high school rewarding. She attended junior college and achieved an associate degree so she could support herself and live independently.

Victor's father left the family when Victor was eight. Mother told stories of how impulsive and violent Father was. Victor learned Father had died after a brawl—he had been treated at an emergency room, but did not follow medical advice. The wound became infected, and he died of complications. Victor was physically abused by Stepfather. Stepfather routinely called Victor "shithead" and would humiliate him in front of friends. One of Victor's worst memories was a Boy Scout canoeing trip where Stepfather, ignoring the vehement objections of the Boy Scout leader and a parent, beat Victor on the head with a paddle and made him sleep in the canoe. Victor tried to get Stepfather's approval and when rebuffed would withdraw into angry brooding. This was repeated hundreds of times during adolescence. As an adult, Victor was prone to repeat this self-defeating pattern. He would try to get Maria's approval, but when rebuffed or something did not go well, Victor would turn on Maria and then sulk, sometimes for hours and sometimes days.

Although Victor and Maria would yell and throw things, they did not hit or push. Even when things were difficult (they experienced job loss and financial problems on an intermittent basis), maintaining a secure home was a strong family imperative. They did disagree about disciplining their four-year-old son and two-year-old daughter. Victor wanted Maria to be like his mother, the children's protector. Maria nurtured their children as well as disciplined them, which is what she asked of Victor. Victor was afraid he would lose his temper, so insisted Maria be the primary parent. Victor was anxious when left alone with both children. Victor believed that the only way he could control children was with spanks and intimidation, but that there were ways a mother could discipline children that a father couldn't.

When Maria would spank their daughter, Victor would scoop her up to get her "out of harm's way." This enraged Maria because she felt Victor thought of her as abusive. Victor knew Maria wasn't an abusive mother, but unconsciously he wanted her to be a "perfect mother," as his mother had been. Maria felt close to her mother-in-law, who was an involved grandparent. One night, after the children were asleep, the three of them discussed parenting. Victor's mother assured him she had gotten angry and spanking was a form of discipline, although she agreed with Maria that time-out was a better disciplinary technique. She told stories of Victor's father and stepfather and how she'd wished her children had a male figure who was involved and nurturing. She urged Victor to be an active, caring father.

They had a heated argument about what was and wasn't physically abusive. Victor wanted it to be black and white and didn't want to discuss it. Maria felt three spanks and yelling was acceptable. Victor's mother was very emotional—at one point defending her parenting, at another saying her grandchildren shouldn't be spanked or yelled at. Maria wanted Victor to attend parenting classes sponsored by the county adult education program. He declined, but agreed to discuss the class and readings with Maria. Victor realized Maria was not a saint, but that she tried to be the best mother she could. Victor was willing to be an involved father, but needed Maria's support and feedback.

They agreed that having a successful family of creation would not be easy, but was more likely to succeed if it were a four-person family. Having three, four, or more children could overwhelm their coping resources. Victor's mother agreed the tradition of larger families did not fit into present realities; it added to the risk of family dysfunction and abuse. Victor worried about the practical, financial, and emotional drains of his family—a third child would overwhelm the system. Victor and Maria agreed that Maria should have a tubal ligation. Maria regretted giving up her fantasy of six children. She was willing to address, talk out, and make plans to avoid the traps of the past, and realized a two-child family would work best. Maria and Victor were not perfect parents nor did they have a perfect family, but they were committed to abstaining from spouse and child abuse. This was a source of pride for them and their family.

THE CHALLENGE, RATHER THAN THE SHAME, OF ABUSE

Adult child literature and groups abound with phrases and terms like overcoming shame, confronting denial, dysfunctional families, co-dependence, victimization. The realities of growing up in a physically violent family, witnessing spouse abuse, being beaten, experiencing emotional abuse or neglect need to be confronted and dealt with. Yet, they cannot become the adult's self-definition. She acknowledges she survived, had positive childhood experiences, and received nurturing from parents or parent substitutes. The majority of people from physically abusive families succeed in creating families free of abuse. It is easy to underestimate the resiliency and strengths of individuals and families. A core survivor concept is to view life as a challenge, rather than determined by past abuse and shame.

Viewing life as a challenge and seeing yourself as a survivor heightens self-esteem. Build a non-violent marriage and family of creation you take pride and satisfaction in. The first step is to realistically assess and accept growing-up experiences, not

feeling shame or stigma even if spouse or child abuse incidents
were frightening and severe. We do not suggest this glibly; we
have heard stories of family violence that were truly horrific,
especially the child's sense of helplessness and hopelessness.
An advantage of being an adult is that you have hope and
resources you didn't as a child. You are not a confused, powerless child, but an aware, responsible adult who can assess and
change her world. You are a survivor who has resources,
alternatives, and the ability to solve problems.

We encourage adults to objectively assess growing-up experiences to see if they were the wastelands depicted in victimization books. No child deserves to be abused, neglected, or to
witness violence. Most children and adults remember nurturing, loving experiences, often from the parent who abused
them. Don't let anger negate positive learnings and experiences. Be aware of the role of parent surrogates, whether aunts
and uncles, grandparents, older siblings, counselors, neighbors, or teachers. To be an adult survivor and successful person, you need to recognize personal strengths and learnings
from childhood and adolescence. What challenges did you
succeed at? Being a survivor includes realistic assessment,
thinking, and gaining perspective about growing up so you can
meet the challenges of adulthood and parenting.

Some readers, an important minority, will hear this and feel
their pain and problems are being minimized. Their childhood
was a violent hellhole where precious little positive happened.
A forty-three-year-old client's first memory was of Father who
had just killed two older siblings coming up the stairs to kill
him and Mother throwing him out the window where he broke
both legs and one arm. Father was found innocent by reason
of insanity and Mother committed suicide. The client grew up
in a series of foster homes, many of which were neglectful.
He'd survived the Vietnam war, married a Cambodian woman,
had a child, and was divorced by twenty-five, losing contact
with his child.

At forty-three, he was married a third time and was a successful computer analyst. His major psychological problems
were impulsive anger, fear of public speaking, and worry this

wife would leave. In therapy, it was crucial to address past abuse, trauma, and neglect, but just as important to learn anger management skills, desensitize speech phobia, and do couple therapy to build a bond of respect, trust, and intimacy.

Therapy was facilitated by awareness that he deserved to be a survivor and live a non-violent life. It was, however, easier for him to learn to control anger than to develop a trusting, intimate marriage. As he reduced shame about childhood and guilt about his first marriage and child, he built a life at forty-three which brought respect and satisfaction. Negative feelings, mistakes, and traumas of his adult years were as serious as childhood abuse.

People who grow up in severely dysfunctional and abusive families are at risk of falling into similar traps in their adult lives. There is clear evidence of the cross-generational transmission of physical violence, alcoholism, poverty, and sexual abuse. However, it is not predestined nor does it occur for the majority of people from dysfunctional families. People can and do function better than their family of origin. This is most likely when they view life as a challenge and do not fall into traps of feeling like a victim or being violent or neglectful to their family of creation.

The person needs strong self-commitment to avoid spouse and child abuse. If there are incidents, he seeks professional intervention and uses family, community, and self-help groups to reverse the pattern. No one is perfect, nor are there perfect marriages and families. The goal is to lead your life in a non-violent manner, and take pride and satisfaction in what you have created. The hope is your children will not have to deal with the demons of abuse so they will create better lives for themselves and their families.

ANGER MANAGEMENT
The traditional "catharsis" theory was that people "stuffed" angry feelings and felt better when they expressed these feelings. The "catharsis" theory of anger is not just

overly simplistic, but empirical research has found it's wrong. The more you express angry feelings the angrier you get. This is truer if the anger is expressed intensely and through physical means. For most people in most circumstances, the more they yell, throw, and hit, the angrier and more out of control they feel. Anger feeds on itself.

This does not mean people should deny or "stuff" angry feelings. Being aware of feelings is a sign of psychological well-being. However, awareness of feelings and appropriate expression of feelings are very different dimensions. Anger management techniques focus on ensuring anger is expressed in a non-abusive manner and is goal-directed rather than self-defeating. It means being aware of feelings, thoughts, and physiological reactions associated with anger, with special attention to feelings of hurt and frustration that underline anger. Express angry feelings and own those feelings, i.e., saying "I'm hurt and angry," not "You did this, so it's your fault I'm angry." "I" statements as opposed to "you" statements are not a semantic technique; it involves taking responsibility for your feelings and behavior.

Anger management entails not acting impulsively or abusively. Anger expression is rational, controlled, and appropriate to what you feel. Rather than an angry attack or counterattack, it is a goal-directed communication. It entails a request to talk out, resolve, and change the source of hurt or frustration. Do not make non-negotiable demands or threaten violence. State the problem, your feelings, and requests for change. Anger is not an intense, out-of-control, impulsive emotion. Anger is a sign of hurt or frustration that needs to be expressed in a clear, direct manner. Anger expression involves requests for change to alleviate the sources of anger, not utilizing demands or intimidation. Anger expression is not about violence or abuse. It is rational, productive, and goal oriented. Anger expression need not accelerate to an out-of-control fight. If it starts becoming out of control, the person has coping techniques to reduce anger, specifically, a time-out period. Anger management techniques are a major resource for the survivor. It allows him to express and deal constructively with anger without becoming abusive or violent. Appropriate anger expression precludes the possibility of spouse and child abuse.

CLOSING THOUGHTS

This was a difficult and draining chapter to write, both intellectually and emotionally. Spouse and child abuse is far too prevalent in our society and does great damage to all involved, especially children. It needs to be confronted, not denied or minimized. The commitment is to non-violent, non-abusive families. As individuals, couples, families, and society, the commitment is to confront domestic violence and work toward nurturing marriages and families. People who have grown up in families where there was spouse and child abuse need to commit to being survivors. The challenge is to use all your resources to create and maintain self-esteem as a non-abusive person and have a marriage and family free of violence. It is not an easy challenge but results in self-respect, satisfaction, and pride in yourself, marriage, and family.

6

INCEST: THE SHAMEFUL FAMILY SECRET

A decade ago people believed incest occurred in one in a million families. Social science researchers have discovered that incestuous incidents (defined as sexual touching involving family members not married to each other, including cousins, siblings, grandparents, uncles, aunts, in-laws, stepsiblings, stepparents, and biological parents) occur in 15–20% of families. Even if cousins, uncles, aunts, and grandparents are eliminated and a narrow definition is used that includes only those living in the home, such as siblings, stepsiblings, live-in boyfriends and girlfriends, stepparents, and parents, the number of families that experience incestuous activity is 5–10%. The majority of incidents involve neither sexual intercourse nor physical force. The most common activities include fondling breasts, exhibitionism, voyeurism, and manual stimulation of genitals. This progresses to intercourse in 20% of cases. Incestuous activity might occur only once or a few times, but more commonly extends over months or years.

When there are incestuous incidents with one daughter, the likelihood is other daughters will be abused. Incidents range from a single experience of genital touching to intercourse which continues for ten years. The most common pattern is incestuous episodes extending over a two-to-four-year period.

Although incest usually does not include physical force or violence, it does involve secrecy and coercion. The majority of victims are girls, although boys are victims in 20% of families. The most common age for incestuous activities is between eight and twelve, but incidents occur with babies, toddlers, teenagers, and young adults. In some families, both sons and daughters are abused. In the vast majority of cases the male is the perpetrator. This is true for both female and male children. For male children 15% of offenders are females, including sisters, stepsisters, cousins, aunts, grandmothers, stepmothers, and mothers.

The majority of incestuous activities are not confronted at the time, but disclosed as adults. This can occur as part of treatment for another problem such as depression, phobias, sexual dysfunction, alcohol or drug abuse, eating disorders, or marital problems. A significant number of women (and an even larger percentage of men) never reveal their "shameful secret." The vast majority of incest victims experience distress or trauma, contrary to the myth that it's an unimportant developmental experience or overplayed by the media and feminist groups.

This brief overview attempts to put incest in a realistic perspective, to "normalize" the experience rather than convey it only happens to "bad people and bad families." This is not to condone or minimize incest and its impact. It is a serious problem that needs to be dealt with so there is not continuing trauma and dysfunction. In therapy, the goal is for the family to confront incest so it does not reoccur and is not the family's defining characteristic.

TYPES OF INCESTUOUS RELATIONSHIPS

There are many causes of incestuous relationships. Let us examine five patterns: (1) part of an alcoholism/chemical abuse problem, (2) part of a dysfunctional family pattern, (3) the man's pedophilia, (4) symptom of the perpetrator's severe mental illness, (5) a sociopathic pattern where the perpetrator sees nothing wrong with incest. The latter two categories are extremely hard to treat and usually result in the dissolution of the family. When there is severe psychopathology, psychiatric treatment or hospitalization is the treatment of choice. The children either remain with the mother, live with more emotionally stable relatives, or are placed in foster care or for adoption. When the incest pattern is sociopathic (antisocial), it is vital to involve the police. The power of law is necessary to halt this type of incest. Usually, the perpetrator is barred from the family and/or is incarcerated.

The great majority of incest families fall in the first three categories. Secrecy and shame permit the sexual abuse to continue. Once the incest is confronted, channels of communication opened, and a therapeutic agreement to facilitate appropriate family roles, incest will almost never reoccur. There needs to be a clear understanding among all family members that incest is unacceptable and will not be tolerated. The secrecy that enabled incest to continue is no longer permissible and any inappropriate sexuality will be confronted.

The subsequent issue as to whether to keep a marriage and family together is an adult decision, not one to be made by children or adolescents (although their feelings need to be listened to). Most important is the child's right not to be subjected to further abuse. Then comes the consideration that children have a right and need to live in a safe, secure home. Usually children want the family to stay together, function better, and for incest and other dysfunctional behavior (alcoholism, spouse abuse, chaos) to cease. Continuing the marriage is a husband-wife decision based on whether the marital bond of respect, trust, and intimacy can be revitalized and the family remain free from abuse. The marital bond is dysfunctional in incest families. The couple has to decide whether their marriage is worth restoring and they can provide a safe, nurturing home for their children.

In alcoholic families, the likelihood of incestuous activity is two-and-a-half times greater than families without chemical dependence. Alcoholism is not an excuse for incest. Successful treatment for alcoholism is necessary to insure incest will not reoccur, but the alcoholic has to commit to abstaining from *both* alcohol and sexually abusive behavior. A relapse in one domain can trigger a relapse in the other. Both problems need to be resolved; treating alcoholism is necessary, but not sufficient.

The typical incestuous family pattern is of a rigid, authoritarian father who blocks lines of communication (secrecy is what allows incest to continue). The mother is often impaired (depressed, physically ill, alcohol or drug dependent, agoraphobic), has low self-esteem, and is not functioning well in the parent role. She is trapped by her problems, avoidant of and intimidated by her husband, and not there emotionally or practically for her children. The oldest daughter is in a "special" position, a confidante of the father, and sees herself as responsible for younger siblings. Incestuous behavior often starts as "special affection," usually nonverbal. As time goes on, touching becomes genital and in some cases proceeds to intercourse. If one child is abused, it's likely other female children will be snared into the incestuous web and, to a lesser extent, male children.

Families where Father, Stepfather, or a relative is a pedophile are more common than previously believed. This is particularly true of stepfamilies where the man is more attracted to the children than his new wife. Pedophiles are likely to offend outside the family as well. They feel more aroused with children than adults. With pedophiles, it is less likely the sexual interaction will include intercourse, but sexual touching causes trauma to children. Perpetrators often minimize the impact by saying, "Since we didn't have intercourse, it wasn't sexual abuse." This rationalization must be confronted. The core of sexual abuse is using the child to meet the adult's sexual needs at the expense of the child's psychological well-being. Successful treatment includes eliminating pedophiliac arousal and building a functional, intimate marital bond.

TREATMENT OF INCEST FAMILIES

Each person from an incest family needs an individual clinical interview. For the child, it allows an empathic, sensitive exploration of sexual development. The child can discuss cognitions and emotions about sexually abusive experiences. The child is believed and feels accepted rather than blamed. She is helped to deal with incest in all its complexity. The broken trust and feelings about victimization are confronted. As well, positive feelings about being special and warm feelings generated by the touching are accepted and acknowledged without feeling guilty or perverse. The child is given a clear message that responsibility for incest lies with the adult. The child did not provoke or maintain incestuous incidents. Incest occurs because it meets inappropriate emotional and sexual needs of the adult.

It was not healthy for the family to deny or pretend incest had not occurred. The child is reassured that revealing the abuse took courage and was the right thing to do. The child receives a clear message that she has a right to control her body. The therapist teaches skills to assert the child's right to protection from abuse and harassment. If sexual touching occurs, the child is urged to immediately tell the mother, a trusted adult, and/or the therapist. The child is taught to be verbally assertive and confrontative, telling the perpetrator sexual touching is abusive and will not be tolerated in silence. Keeping channels of communication open and not allowing a return to secrecy is the major antidote to incest. The child is encouraged to restore communication and trust with siblings and the mother. Incest is something to be confronted, dealt with, and overcome, not to be the controlling family secret.

It is important the child understand the decision of whether to keep the marriage and family together is for parents to make, not her. The child has a right to be in a safe environment and not be revictimized or made to feel guilty or blamed. The perpetrator cannot deny or minimize. He needs to admit responsibility and commit to abstain from abusive behavior. He needs treatment for alcoholism, pedophilia, depression, or other problems that promoted incestuous activity. The couple needs to reestablish its marital bond and family members have to work together to improve functioning. Mother can be a strong force in the family as she rebuilds self-esteem and trust with her children. Father needs to understand he cannot remain in the house if he is physically or sexually abusive. If the family is to remain intact, incest has to be effectively dealt with and the possibility of reoffending blocked (in fact, incest has a very low recidivism rate). The family has to practice open communication, problem solving, and emotional cohesion. They view themselves as a family which has successfully confronted incest, not as a stigmatized family, controlled by the shameful secret of incest.

The final therapy session (here, dealing hypothetically with incest between Father and a daughter) centers on a structured apology. Father says what motivated him to engage in incestuous behavior, takes responsibility for it, does not blame the child, apologizes for the behavior, and tells the child his hopes for her. She then has a chance to ask him any questions and say what she wants. When she accepts the apology, she agrees to not use incest as an excuse or weapon in the future. After Father has apologized to each child (including those with whom there was no sexual contact), Mother speaks to each child. She apologizes for not being there emotionally for her children, assures them she will not tolerate any abusive behavior in the future, and says how she feels about the child. Each child has a chance to ask questions of Mother, say what they want, and then accept the apology. Incest can be discussed but not used as a weapon or manipulation by either the adult or the child. The family is followed at six-month intervals for two years. Each member knows, if a problem occurs, they can call and it will be addressed. Dealing with individual, couple, and family problems is crucial for healthy functioning.

This description of a successfully treated incest family is the optimal intervention. About 60% of these families stay together. In most families incest is best dealt with as a therapeutic issue, not a legal one. In families where parents separate, it is crucial Mother not blame the children for the divorce. Well-functioning single-parent families are much superior to dysfunctional intact families. Mother needs to build self-esteem and be a nurturing parent. Rather than feeling stigmatized by the incest and divorce, she sees herself as a survivor and utilizes available resources (extended family, therapy, self-help groups) to rebuild her life and facilitate the children's development.

Adults who experienced incest may read this discourse with a sense of pain. They ask, "Why couldn't this have happened to me and my family? Why did I have to keep this secret and feel I was bad and to blame? Why was there not public awareness and therapy programs when I was a child?"

Therapeutic interventions with incest families are still at a very early stage. Many children encounter the other side of the pendulum swing—involvement with social service agencies, police, the court system—experiencing a different type of victimization and stigma. As adults, they will have to deal with a different set of pain and trauma. Confronting the reality of incest is far superior to denying it, but for a truly healing intervention, the feelings and needs of all family members must be listened to in a respectful, caring manner.

Survivors of incest report that as children they had a great need to talk to someone to help them understand and deal with what happened. For the great majority, incest is not dealt with at the time. What brings the adult incest victim into therapy are problems such as alcohol or drug abuse, depression, phobias, sexual dysfunction (especially inhibited sexual desire, sexual aversion, or non-orgasmic response), and marital or parenting problems. Confronting incest helps the victims become survivors. With increased awareness and empowerment, they can deal more effectively with life issues. The key is not denying or letting incest control their life, but accepting the reality and seeing themselves as survivors. They deserve the self-esteem and sexuality which enhances an intimate relationship.

INCEST BOOKS AND SELF-HELP GROUPS

The last decade has seen an explosion of books and 12-step groups for incest victims. The strength of self-help books and groups is to help confront denial and provide emotional support and validation. The weakness is the focus on anger and self-defeating advice about confrontation with the perpetrator and other family members. The danger of this is revictimization. The outcome of many of these confrontations is emotional cutoff, not only from the perpetrator but other family members. The black-and-white "you're-either-with-me-or-against-me" approach ignores the incredible complexity of family dynamics, both at the time of incest and in adulthood. Rather than becoming a survivor, many of the books and groups promote the angry victim who denounces her past and family. Anger is part of the healing process, but being controlled by anger is almost as detrimental as being controlled by guilt and shame.

Women (there are almost no groups for males) who attend 12-step incest survivor groups have mixed reactions. The most positive and universal experience is the relief of being able to tell your story, be believed, and feel emotionally supported. Crying in the group and receiving hugs and being told "you're all right" is powerfully validating.

Many self-help groups expect the woman to make either a lifelong commitment to "working the program" or at least a year's commitment to attend every group meeting (whether weekly or three times a week). This is an inordinate commitment of time and energy. If they refuse, they are accused of being in "denial." This one-track righteous push induces guilt and low self-esteem. The program takes precedence over the individual.

Guidelines for adults in self-help groups include 1) maintain a sense of personal responsibility, 2) judge what is right for her, and 3) adopt components that enhance recovery and well-being. Trust your instincts and reject aspects of the program or group that are not right for you. The incest survivor can use resources—individual, couple, family or group psychotherapy, sexual abuse books, sexuality groups—to help in the complex process of healing. It is the individual who must judge what is helpful and what is not.

The McDonald Family. Sixteen-year-old Judy broke down in front of her high-school guidance counselor. Through heaving sobs, she revealed her father had made her manually and orally stimulate him to orgasm. Judy had not planned to reveal this, but the pressure of carrying the secret for three years had become overwhelming. The guidance counselor had a legal mandate to report the abuse to the county child protective service agency. The counselor called Mother and made a strong plea for family therapy so the family would receive therapeutic help rather than be stuck in the web of the social service and legal system.

All family members—which included fourteen-year-old Alan and twelve-year-old Alice, as well as Mother, Father, and Judy—were requested to attend the initial family therapy session. The McDonald family was in crisis and the therapist wanted to move quickly before defensiveness and anger blocked progress. It was crucial Judy and her siblings feel safe and their needs and rights be protected. Mother was intelligent, but drained by multiple sclerosis and panicked by Judy's accusations. Father appeared both frightened and angry, fighting to maintain self-respect and control. He admitted to personal and family problems, but denied he'd ever hurt his children. In incest cases, if the social worker suspects an incident has occurred, the child is removed from the home to protect her from further abuse. This means leaving friends and entering a different school, which is viewed by the child as a punishment. If possible, it is the perpetrator who leaves the home. In the family session, Mr. McDonald was asked if he cared enough for his family to live with a relative on a temporary basis until the problems could be assessed and an intervention developed which would benefit all family members. He reluctantly agreed. The family was assured each person's needs and family problems would be addressed by the female-male co-therapy team.

All five family members were given individual appointments for a sexual history interview. What emerged was that Mr. McDonald had a pedophiliac arousal pattern and had sexually abused both daughters and other children. Like most pedophiles, this pattern had existed since adolescence. He was ashamed, but felt hopeless about a compulsive, addictive behavior he couldn't control. With potential legal liability as the stick and desire to retain his marriage and family as the carrot, Mr. McDonald agreed to individual therapy and a sexual addiction self-help group. Mr. McDonald's treatment focused on eliminating deviant arousal, increasing sexual information and comfort, awareness of the negative effects of sexual abuse, and commitment to an intimate, sexually functional marriage.

Mrs. McDonald was devastated by the revelation, but realized her husband's problems were severe and long-standing. Although they'd remained an affectionate couple, they had not been sexual for five years. She'd blamed the sexual dysfunction on herself and the low energy caused by her illness. She was appalled to learn he'd acted out against Judy and Alice and that this had been going on for years.

Judy was feeling both relieved and guilty. Was this going to destroy her family? Adolescence is a difficult enough period without having to deal with the trauma of incest. Judy believed engaging sexually with Father was protecting the family and was devastated to learn Alice had been sexually abused for the past two years. Alice was very needy and the least well-functioning of the children. She was eager to be in individual therapy. At times Judy and Mother came to sessions. One of the most emotional sessions was with Judy and Alice where they pledged to stay sisters and friends. Alan had not been abused, but did feel neglected and abandoned by the family. Alan loved his parents, but they seemed so unhappy and overwhelmed. One of the most helpful interventions involved Alan's taking a supportive role with Judy and Alice. Alan developed a close relationship with his sisters. Alan told Father he respected and loved him, but hated the sexual abuse and vowed he would not abuse women.

Family therapy is the treatment of choice for incest. It is very complex and seldom easy. Sessions with Mr. and Mrs. McDonald emphasized the importance of building a genuine marital bond of respect, trust, and intimacy. The responsibility for incest lies with the perpetrator, not the spouse, but the spouse has an active role in rebuilding the marriage and family. Mrs. McDonald's passivity inadvertently facilitated incestuous activity. Mrs. McDonald needed to live with the reality of her multiple sclerosis, but had to be an active person, spouse, and parent. This meant challenging inhibited sexual desire and sexual avoidance. It also meant being strong enough so that if there was inappropriate sexual touching or other abuse, the daughters could tell her and trust she would act in their best interest. She had to be strong enough to insist Mr. McDonald leave if they couldn't have a home safe from abuse.

Judy needed to regain personal and sexual integrity. She enjoyed writing and greatly benefited from the exercises assigned as part of therapy. Putting her thoughts and feelings on paper made it clear it was healthy and necessary for her family to confront incest. She mourned the loss of childhood innocence, but felt more aware and responsible than the typical adolescent. She wanted sexuality to be a positive, integral part of her adult life.

Alice benefited from the support and attention, but continued to struggle with body-image issues. Much of the incestuous activity had involved her hands and breasts, which she viewed as ugly parts of her. She chose to keep distant from boys and not engage in the "puppy love" interaction appropriate for her age. Mother once again became Alice's confidante.

The McDonald family was followed on a six-month basis for two years with additional sessions scheduled as needed. Theirs is not a "perfect family" story, but they were a better functioning, more nurturing family. There were no further sexual incidents. Incest damages a family and its individual members, but the McDonald family survived and moved beyond incest.

NON-PARENTAL INCEST

The majority of incest experiences involve cousins, siblings, stepfathers, uncles, step-brothers, in-laws, grandfathers. These are usually less traumatic than father-daughter incest, but a significant trust bond is broken. The offender has to be confronted, not allowed to minimize by saying it was "normal fooling around." Parents need to be clear they will not tolerate abusive sexual behavior. The key is assertive confrontation, not allowing secrecy. The child or adolescent deserves to live in a sexually safe environment.

Incest involves intrafamily age and power differences that meet the older or more powerful person's sexual needs at the expense of the child or adolescent. Incestuous experiences and reactions are very individualistic. Usually, sibling and cousin incidents are less traumatic than those involving uncles or older relatives. Some believe these experiences are in the range of normal sex play and exploration, not exploitative or abusive. The trauma of incest is defined by both behavioral experiences and subjective evaluations. We are not trying to create victims or trauma where none exists.

Sexually abusive behavior includes incidents a seventeen-year-old stepbrother calls sex play with his eleven-year-old stepsister, but is clearly exploitative. He feels sexually excited, but it causes her confusion, guilt, and negative feelings. The younger person believes the older person would not hurt her and has her best interests in mind. The trust broken by this abusive sexual behavior is that he puts his sexual needs over her emotional needs. Incidents of sexual humiliation and harassment occur with disturbing frequency in the extended family. The adult survivor of cousin or stepsibling incest needs to reassert his right to a voluntary, intimate, pleasurable sexual relationship, where his emotional and sexual needs are treated with respect. Abuse is prevalent among male cousins, siblings, and stepsiblings. The stigma and confusion caused by same-sex abuse is the most difficult legacy.

Many families have major misconceptions about male-female roles and sexuality. The traditional assumption is that males and females are very different. Males need to be powerful and dominant, and a "real man is able and willing to have sex any time, any place, with any woman." Incest and rape are the extreme example of male dominance. The woman is viewed as weak; it's her role to do whatever is necessary to keep the marriage and family together. She is a sex object, not a sexual person. The scientific reality is there are many more similarities than differences between men and woman. Men need to be aware of their responsibility to treat women (especially in their family) in respectful, caring ways. Women need to assert personal and sexual rights. Families where incest occurs do not have a model of appropriate affection among family members or clear guidelines about adult/child emotional boundaries. When males identify touching as sexual, there is either no touching with daughters, sisters, cousins, and nieces—or touching is sexually abusive.

There is not a thin line or gray area between affectionate touching and sexually abusive touching—they are very different. Affectionate touching involves a voluntary, friendly, warm, non-erotic, positive contact with another person. Sexually abusive touching involves a hidden agenda, meeting the male's needs at the expense of the girl's, use of age or power differences to get his way, sex as manipulation and coercive behavior, and lack of concern for the girl's feelings. Appropriate affection between a male and female relative is an affirmation of caring, an expression of valuing that person. One of the most harmful effects of incest is it negates the positive human experience of touching. Incest breaks trust and is a gross misuse of touching.

In well-functioning families, there is a clear boundary between generations and recognition of the value of communication. Incest families have a rigid, authoritarian system, lack of respect and, most important, absence of open communication. The male claims to be superior and in command, but under this thin facade he feels vulnerable and incompetent. He needs to govern with an iron hand because he feels unloved and insecure. His force comes not from strength, but from weakness. Women suffer from a lack of power and withdraw. When you scratch the surface of these families, you discover fears and dysfunction.

INCEST INVOLVING MALE CHILDREN

Incest is a special stigma for the male child. In the large majority of cases, the perpetrator is male—father, stepfather, grandfather, older brother, uncle, cousin, in-law. In addition to the broken trust, the boy has to deal with the issue of same-sex abuse. Males are supposed to be in control. The boy feels humiliated; his masculinity has been compromised. Sexual interaction tends to be forceful and intrusive, often involving fellatio and/or anal intercourse. The boy is usually passive in anal intercourse and the one performing fellatio, but even if the roles are reversed, it is the boy who is coerced or forced to meet the adult's sexual needs. If the boy becomes aroused and orgasmic the man will say he wanted sex, so he loses either way. Boys are less likely to reveal sexual abuse than girls, especially intrafamily incidents. When sex is assaultive, there is further stigma and an added burden. If the father (stepfather, uncle, grandfather, etc.) is a pedophile, revealing incest will reverberate in significant ways. The man who offends against relatives is likely to offend against children outside the family.

Male children who are incest victims and their families are in need of professional intervention, but do not receive it. Even if the secret is revealed, professionals operate under the same misinformation as the public, so often are not empathic or helpful. The child needs understanding, acceptance, and support to deal with his complex emotions and thoughts about the incidents, the perpetrator and, most importantly, feelings about masculinity and sexuality. The crucial issue is whether the young male blames himself for the sexual incidents or mislabels their occurrence as a sign he "thought I was gay." As with all incidents of child sexual abuse, the responsibility lies with the perpetrator not the victim/survivor. The perpetrator did not pick his victim because he knew something about him sexually, but because the child was accessible and vulnerable. This says nothing about the survivor's worth or sexual orientation.

The great majority of young men with a history of incest are and continue to be heterosexual. The most victimized are those whose sexual orientation is homosexual. Rather than accepting homosexuality and leading a successful gay life, they often feel stigmatized that the incestuous experience caused them to be homosexual. For those whose sexual orientation is homosexual, they need to accept being gay is optimal for them and commit to being successful gay people.

It is crucial to regain sexual self-esteem and not feel controlled by the incestuous experience. The process is similar to that of female survivors, with added emphasis on sharing the secret with at least one person (often a female, most commonly his wife or partner). It is important to see sex as a means of expressing pleasure and intimacy, not as coercion or meeting someone else's needs. He can feel comfortable and confident as a sexual person. It is crucial not to fall into the trap of proving one's masculinity by having sex with as many women as possible or sexually abusing children (over 50% of pedophiles were themselves sexually abused). Feeling good about being a sexual man is a psychological process of awareness and acceptance.

SURVIVING INCEST

If incest is viewed as the most important experience in the person's life, he or she will continue to be a victim. A negative experience should never be a primary self-definition. Awareness and commitment to sexuality which affirms personal integrity and enhances an intimate relationship is the hallmark of a survivor. Shame, guilt, and blame are of no benefit. The survivor did not cause incest. It is in her best interest to view the incestuous experiences in the least pejorative and blaming way possible. As with the rape survivor, the incest survivor needs to be aware "living well is the best revenge."

The incest survivor has the special issue of broken trust and needs to deal with family members. The most helpful guideline is to make choices which enhance self-esteem and promote self-respect. Establishing an intimate marriage and a healthy family of creation is a symbol of surviving incest.

7
DANGERS OF PARENT BASHING

In the past ten years, books on Adult Children have engaged in an orgy of parent blaming for psychological, sexual, addictive, and relational problems. It's presented as a black-and-white issue: parents are totally at fault for any and all problems of adult children. If you grew up in an alcoholic or dysfunctional family, the inevitable result is dysfunctional adults and the fault lies with parents.

It is easy to blame the "bad guys," but does this help the adult child become a responsible, loving human being? The answer is an unequivocal no. Parent bashing might make you feel better for awhile, but doesn't help you become a survivor. In fact, it reinforces being a victim caught in the trap of blaming and low self-esteem. You might be an angry victim rather than a passive victim, but nonetheless you're a victim. Parent blamers are destined to lead lives burdened by the past.

An example of being caught in the parent-blaming trap is a woman who ranted against her alcoholic father who had been physically and sexually abusive. In addition to individual therapy, she was in four 12-step groups dealing with childhood trauma. However, she would not deal with present problems, specifically her alcoholism and its effect on her children. She was so angry at her father's past victimization, she had no psychological energy or desire to deal with her own life. Her alcoholism was a revictimization which caused her children (she was custodial parent after a divorce) to grow up in an alcoholic, neglectful home. The cross-generational legacy of alcoholism and family dysfunction is a tragedy that is repeated in many families, in this case, exacerbated by the woman's focus on her history of abuse and anger at the abusive parent.

When should you stop blaming parents? When you are eighteen? Twenty-one? Thirty? When you have children of your own? Never? Growing up in an alcoholic, dysfunctional, abusive, or neglectful family is a burden. Responsibility for family dysfunction lies with the parents. The child engaging in self-blame because of a dysfunctional family is neither rational nor productive. The adult needs to accept the reality of abusive and deficit growing-up experiences and realistically assess their multicausal nature. Being a survivor includes acknowledging positive learnings and nurturing experiences provided by parents or parent surrogates.

The usual approach is to think of parents as an inseparable team—"the parents"—or split them into dichotomous roles—"Father was a brute, Mother was a saint." It's easy, simplistic, black-and-white thinking, and usually untrue. The parent is first a person, with his or her strengths and weaknesses. There were times when both parents acted in concert; other times their approaches were quite different. We tend to remember extremes, not the complicated nuances and shades of gray. Parents were not the same for twenty years—at times their lives were in order and parenting was adequate and even good. Other times their lives were out of control (heavy drinking, psychosis, depression, anger) and parenting abusive and dysfunctional. A child's memories are more black and white than the reality. It is the world through the eyes of a child or adolescent—a very different viewpoint from objective facts. It is difficult to pick up a magazine and not find an article that bashes Mother for being overinvolved with her children or bashes Father for being distant and unavailable. We are a culture that currently revels in parent bashing.

Parent bashing, however, subverts the person's self-esteem

and is a roadblock to a healthy, functional family of creation. Parent bashing distracts the person from focusing on adult life. Blaming parents causes shame about family of origin and diverts attention and energy from the family of creation. Negative motivation, especially shame, guilt, and blaming, interferes with people's lives and families.

A PERSONAL NOTE

During the writing of this chapter my seventy-nine-year-old father, Edward, died. As I attended the wake and funeral, talked to relatives, and divided up old photos, a host of memories and feelings came back. Edward had been an angry man, given to violent outbursts. Most of the time he was silent and emotionally distant, but his unpredictable anger intimidated family members and others.

Edward was minimally involved with the adult lives of me and my sister. He did not understand my profession and never read the books I had written, but was proud I had an independent life and family. Edward was supportive in terms of practical and financial matters, although not emotionally or verbally expressive.

As an adult, I tried to talk to Edward about his life and mine. Edward was a secretive, self-contained person who did not disclose perceptions or feelings. At the wake, I heard stories of how controlling my grandfather was and, as the last of ten children, how little nurturing Edward received. Much emotion was tied to traumatic experiences during World War II and anger and obsessing over his job. Fear of losing control was the motivation for his need for order and routine.

As I developed my life and career and married and had children, I was able to view my parents in a mature, rational perspective. I realized they were people first, with genuine strengths and painful vulnerabilities. Edward was a responsible, dependable person, respected at his job, helpful to others, religious, supported his family financially, and was well-intentioned. My mother, Dorothy, who died seventeen years before her husband, was a bright, creative person, socially active, overly focused on caretaking, and an excellent craftswoman. On the negative side, my parents had a very dysfunctional marriage. Tensions about personal and marital problems pervaded the family. Dorothy was intimidated by Edward's anger, and this further lowered her self-esteem. She had heart problems caused by childhood rheumatic fever. Edward's fears were exacerbated by her poor health—that he'd be stuck parenting two children, a task for which he had neither skill nor interest. I was the target of Edward's anger and physical abuse. My younger sister felt overwhelmed and depressed, trying to take responsibility for the family. It was a tense, dysfunctional family.

As an adult, I kept moderate contact, and felt sadness for my parents and their lives. Emily and I were strongly committed to having an intimate, communicative marriage and a non-abusive, nurturing family of creation. One of our first agreements was to not live in Illinois where we would be burdened on a daily basis by family tensions. Dorothy died when our oldest son was five. Edward remarried. My stepmother, a very nice person and an excellent grandmother, was an important figure in our children's lives; but Edward was an emotionally distant grandfather.

Two days after the funeral, I took my youngest son, Paul, an eighteen-year-old college freshman, on a walk around Chicago to see where Edward had grown up and worked. I told Paul a number of stories about Edward and tried to answer Paul's questions. Edward kept many things secret. I was determined to share information, perceptions, and feelings with my children. I felt I'd done a better job parenting and encouraged Paul to avoid traps and be a better parent to his future children. This is how people and families become more functional and loving.

ACCEPTANCE AND FORGIVENESS

Accept the reality of childhood and focus psychological energy on building self-esteem, an intimate marriage, and a loving, functional family. Accepting parents as people with deficiencies and vulnerabilities helps this process. Identify strengths to incorporate in your life. Carefully monitor traps so they are not repeated in your life and family of creation.

If you don't repeat abusive patterns, issues from the past are easier to accept and deal with. The most vociferous parent blamers are those who feel out of control in their adult lives. Parental abuse is a major factor in causing problems, but the parent cannot cure the problems. The adult needs to use all his resources to avoid traps of abuse and dysfunction. Blaming parents puts the focus on the past—it needs to be on the present and future.

Andrea. Twenty-eight-year-old Andrea was an important member of the Adult Children of Alcoholics (ACOA) group and sponsored five people. She was well-read in Adult Child issues, a dynamic speaker at meetings, well liked and highly regarded. Andrea was a model group member. People admired how she could express feelings of pain and rage. She no longer "stuffed" feelings nor did she cover up the trauma caused by alcoholism and child and spouse abuse.

Andrea's father died of a heart attack when she was twenty-three. Alcoholism played a major role in his ill health and death. Father had been hospitalized twice, once in a thirty-day inpatient alcoholism program and the second time for ten days in a psychiatric hospital. Neither time did Father follow the AA program for more than a month. As a teenager, Andrea attended Alateen, went to Al-Anon with Mother, and for the past three years was active in ACOA.

Andrea had convinced her thirty-one-year-old sister and brother-in-law to attend ACOA meetings, but neither her twenty-four-year-old brother nor his fiancée was interested. The brother felt there would be too much whining and complaining at meetings. When the three siblings talked about their family they shared horror stories and cried. Andrea believed it was crucial to confront the pain of childhood and express the anger and tears they were not allowed as children. She was sure the road to recovery was confronting the pain, but unsure of how to proceed past that. Arguments with siblings and their partners confused her. Andrea was not in a relationship at the time. She believed adult children of alcoholics often chose unhealthy relationships, especially women who become involved with alcohol-abusing men. Andrea was an independent, aware woman who didn't need a man to validate her.

Andrea had lunch with her brother's fiancée. She told Andrea they'd entered couples premarital counseling. She realized achieving a successful marriage would require work and communication, in part because of Andrea's brother's family background and difficulty expressing emotions. She suggested that perhaps Andrea could benefit from individual therapy to explore her reluctance to trust in intimate relationships.

Andrea first consulted a feminist therapist who surprised her by suggesting it would be therapeutic to work with a male therapist with expertise in adults from dysfunctional families. Andrea found psychotherapy more emotionally challenging and difficult than 12-step groups. While she appreciated the empathy and careful listening of the therapist, she was jarred by his comments and questions about what she had learned from childhood and how it affected self-esteem and relationships. Her pat lines from Adult Children groups were not dismissed, but the therapist continued to question and probe. Andrea became aware her life and relationships were full of crises and support, but little joy or intimacy. She had a number of male buddies, males she sponsored, and men she occasionally had sex with, but no genuine emotional or sexual intimacy. Andrea was proud she avoided abusive relationships, but missed the warmth and joy of an intimate relationship. The therapist observed she was so wary of the past she didn't trust herself to live in the present.

This was true not only of relationships, but her work. Andrea was a graphic illustrator whose career was stagnant. So much time and energy went to the victimization/recovery process, the marketing plan her supervisor asked for was ten months overdue. It had been over a year since she'd gotten a raise.

The most difficult element in therapy was talking about parents. The therapist listened to family stories in an empathic manner. He did not want her to deny or minimize abuse and emotional pain, but did want her to focus on learnings. This was a difficult perspective. Ever since Andrea was a child she thought of parents in a black-and-white manner. The exercise listing positive and negative characteristics of Mother and Father took three weeks to complete. Viewing Father as a person with positive and negative characteristics, a parent with strengths and weaknesses, and assessing positive learnings was extremely difficult. It's harder to bash and blame a complex person than a simplistic symbol. Asking Andrea to view Mother and the marriage from a multidimensional perspective was almost as difficult. What had Andrea learned about respect, trust, and intimacy? This level of analysis and confrontation with assumptions, beliefs, perceptions, and feelings had been ignored in the Adult Child groups and readings. Andrea was in touch with feelings about abuse, anger, blaming, and the unfairness and trauma of growing up. She was unaware of strengths, respect for resiliency, positive learnings from childhood, parents as people, fatal flaws of the marriage. Most important, she was unaware of what she needed to be a survivor and create healthy, stable relationships. Andrea realized she had a lot of work ahead of her in therapy, but felt on the right track.

Andrea continued to attend one or two ACOA meetings a month and encouraged new members, but stopped sponsoring. Andrea felt she'd achieved maximum benefit from the group and, as her brother said, it was time to move on to the next chapter of her life. She continued individual therapy to build awareness, insights, and skills. Andrea realized she couldn't change her parents or the past and needed to focus energy on the present, self-esteem, and relationships. Most of her friends were in 12-step programs and much of their conversation was about abuse and dysfunction. Andrea wanted to develop new interests and friends as well as put energy into her career. She joined the local professional graphics organization and was appointed liaison to the marketing committee. The newly freed-up nights allowed her to join a volleyball league and tutoring program for disadvantaged children.

She was discerning in choosing new friendships. She believed happily single was preferable to being unhappily married, but was open to a serious relationship. Andrea did something she swore she'd never do—put a personal ad in the "In Search Of" section of a local magazine. She met men for lunch or coffee dates. She trusted her intuition on which men to avoid.

Andrea reported better relationships with her siblings and their families. More conversations were about the present, less about past trauma. They discovered a pride in adult accomplishments and personal growth. Conversations about parents were less confrontational and more reflective. There was greater emphasis on utilizing insights to build competencies and avoid falling into old traps. Siblings supporting each other's growth and strengths was of great value. Andrea had outgrown the need to blame and bash parents.

Exercise—Acceptance, Not Blaming

This is the time to reflect on attitudes toward your parents. We suggest dividing this exercise into three sections: attitudes toward parents when growing up, adult attitudes toward parents, and forgiveness. Although this can be done alone, it would be better to discuss this with siblings, good friends, or spouse (if they are positive and supportive).

Review childhood experiences with the benefit of insights and perspectives as a mature adult. Avoid being simplistic and parent bashing. Be aware of the reality of traumatic or abusive incidents, including painful, humiliating, and depressing experiences. Focus on specific incidents of fathering and mothering that were hurtful, confusing, or negative. Remember the ages and specific words, actions, and circumstances. What were your thoughts, feelings, and behavior at the time of the incidents? What caused the incidents? How did you understand Father's actions? Mother's actions? Were you the cause of the anger or was it something else—a marital fight, parents' personal problems, reaction to situational stress, a psychosis? How do these insights change your reactions to the abusive or traumatic incidents? How were the incidents dealt with—were there discussions or an apology? Did similar incidents happen to siblings or were they unique to you?

As an adult, what are your attitudes toward Mother and Father (or stepparent)? Are your parents still alive and married? How much contact do you have with them? Do you discuss issues from the past? Do you see them as people with strengths and weaknesses? Or are they stuck forever in the freeze-frame of being parents to the traumatized child? Do you have a mature adult relationship or is it controlled by blaming? Is the relationship shrouded in silence and controlled by guilt or are angrily hurled accusations and counterattacks the coin of exchange? The ideal, which no one is likely to reach, is to see one's parents as unique individuals who conveyed a complex legacy. Appreciate positive learnings and experiences while confronting traps and dysfunctions, with a commitment to not repeat the negative experiences in your family of creation. Accepting the parents for who they are and understanding the forces influencing them (family of origin, pressures, angst and anger, fear and depression, addiction or psychosis, rigidity or unrealism, poverty or worthlessness) gives you a clearer view of them—and yourself.

Equally important is to understand the marriage—a prime root of family dysfunction and child abuse is a non-respectful, non-loving marriage. The couple are in conflict with children caught in the middle. Children become unwitting pawns in the parents' unhappiness. Rather than diverting psychological energy by blaming parents, adults who had a poor marital and/or parental model need to develop a respectful, trusting, intimate marriage and nurturing family. What is your under-standing of your parents and their marriage? How much of your energy is spent on guilt, blame, and shame from the past and how much on understanding and acceptance in the present?

In assessing the adult relationship with each parent, the crucial question is whether acceptance or blaming is in your best interest. There are cases where a person who had been physically and sexually abused by Father and has chosen to have no contact with him. The person views him as a violent, sad, or sociopathic human being whose pattern he is committed not to repeat. Hate, blaming, shame, and guilt, however, do not promote healthy goals. The person might never forgive Father, but accepts the reality of a traumatic childhood while focusing energy and taking pride in a life of non-violence.

The focus of this exercise is to see one's parents and their marriage in a realistic perspective, which includes positive learnings and experiences. Negating these does not punish your parents, but is self-punishing. Be proud of the strengths of parents, relatives, parent surrogates, teachers, or friends; it is a part of your legacy. Accepting positive experiences does not mean denying or minimizing abuse or dysfunction. This gives a clearer, multidimensional perspective to your family of origin.

The last part of the exercise involves forgiveness. Those from religious backgrounds might remember going to a priest, rabbi, or minister, disclosing sins and misdeeds and feeling that God can forgive you. Leaving the meeting or confessional, the person felt unburdened and resolved to lead her life in a healthier, more productive manner. The weight of guilt and blame was lifted. The goal of this exercise is to similarly lift the burden of silence, guilt, and blame. One way to reduce the weight of the past is to understand and forgive one's parent or parents. Anger and blame are heavy burdens. Is forgiveness for certain acts or in general? Is the forgiveness because you understand the parent did not mean harm and did the best she could? Or because even though the parent was mean and destructive you choose to forgive her?

Forgiveness is a psychological choice, sometimes accompanied by a specific act such as writing a letter or having a serious talk with the parent. Letters are usually not sent, they are written for yourself. The unsent letter is a way to resolve feelings about a dead parent. Be aware that sending a letter or having a confrontative talk with a parent can be draining and disruptive. Before doing this consider the following:

1. Your motivation is to forgive and reduce the weight; not be hostile, evoke defensiveness, or fight about the past.

2. What you want from the parent. An acknowledgment
and apology is the best you can reasonably expect. Many
people want parents to beg for forgiveness, make a complete
and full apology, and offer money or another payback. That
is unlikely.

3. Prepare yourself for a negative response. Many parents
become defensive and counterattack. It is very hard to parent
one's parents even in the best of circumstances. Don't allow
yourself to be dragged back into the guilt and blame of the
past. Retain your integrity and focus—to forgive, not to
refight old battles.

SANDWICHED BETWEEN YOUR PARENTS AND YOUR CHILDREN

It's preferable to come to grips with the past in your twenties
before beginning your family. It's easy to imagine establishing
your marriage and family (and doing much better than your
parents), but extremely difficult to imagine dealing with aging
parents. The role reversal (parenting your parents) is mind-
boggling for even the most functional adults.

Your family of creation deserves and needs more time and
psychological energy than your family of origin. Life is meant
to be lived in the present, not controlled by resentment or
compensation for the past. This guideline has particular rele-
vance in dealing with aging parents. The multiple demands of
adulthood—job, house, spouse, parenting, community,
friends, and aging parents—is a difficult juggling act. For most
people the priorities are 1) personal well-being, 2) marriage,
3) parenting, and 4) supporting aging parents. This is not a
punishment of parents, but a recognition of life realities. During a crisis these priorities can and do change.

Adults who have dealt with the problems of growing up and
have established a mature relationship with parents are in a
better position to make decisions and establish priorities. It is
easier to deal with aging parents about present issues and needs
that are not contaminated by old issues, guilt, or resentments.

Remember, the past cannot be undone. People driven by negative motivation—guilt, retribution, trying to achieve parental
approval—are unlikely to make good decisions or follow
through on plans. Adults with positive motivation—whether
altruism, providing family contact and support, loyalty, doing
the right thing, a model for children—will act constructively
and follow through. It is not, however, in your best interest to
promise heroic action for parents or sacrifice everything for
them. You'll wind up resenting them and feeling guilty because
you didn't deliver what you promised. You'll resent the burden
and feel cheated when the parent doesn't become the all-loving,
all-accepting person you wish he had been during your childhood.

ELDER ABUSE

One of the reasons for the growing, but underreported, incidents of elder abuse is that people are living longer, and adults
are having to take care of parents they don't want or can't
handle. Anger and resentment from the past are often acted
out in abusive incidents. For the sake of the aging parent
as well as the adult child, it would be better to face reality
beforehand. Adults often feel so angry and alienated from
parents they cannot be caregivers. People should not take on
what they cannot comfortably and competently do; otherwise
they court disaster—a continuation of the abuse cycle. Revenge via elder abuse makes no sense psychologically, legally,
or any other way; not to mention damage to your spouse's and
children's view of you. Elder abuse is never justified by child
abuse. The way to overcome victimization is not by being a
perpetrator of violence and abuse.

CLOSING THOUGHTS

There are two major themes in this chapter—1) parent bashing does not help a person deal with abuse and dysfunction of
the past and become a survivor responsible for his life and

family of creation; and 2) understanding, acceptance, forgiveness, and a commitment to not repeat the pattern is the healthy response. The more you accept each parent as a person with his or her strengths and weaknesses, and accept your growing up with both its positives and negatives, the more you are a survivor.

8
ACCEPTING THE REALITY
OF YOUR CHILDHOOD

This is the most important chapter for adults dealing with childhood abuse and trauma. The challenge is to accept your childhood in a manner which promotes adult self-esteem and healthy functioning. The key is viewing yourself as a survivor, not a victim.

The Adult Child movement brought public attention to issues of abuse, trauma, and damage caused by growing up in families controlled by alcoholism, physical violence, sexual abuse, and/or neglect. These are real issues and bringing them out of the shadows and silence was of great benefit. Unspoken, painful realities can now be addressed. However, any psychological concept taken to an extreme can be destructive, especially the victimization mindset of the Adult Child movement.

The reason to confront dysfunctional families and victimization is to increase awareness and empowerment to deal with present life issues, not to celebrate abuse and trauma. One's primary self-definition being a negative event—"I am an adult child of incest," "The most important thing about me is I grew up in an alcoholic family," or "I was an abused child"—is self-defeating. These experiences are a part of you, but not your self-definition. Theoretically, clinically, and personally, we believe self-esteem should never be defined by a negative.

People whose primary self-definition is as an Adult Child are being victimized by this as much as, if not more than, childhood abuse.

Psychological well-being begins by accepting and dealing with reality. Accept the challenge of being a survivor rather than wallow in the guilt and shame of feeling like a victim. Establish a sense of pride about what you have achieved and experienced, both in childhood and adulthood. People devastated by childhoods where they were repeatedly beaten or subjected to ritualistic abuse and adulthoods where they were hospitalized, imprisoned, and had numerous failures and rejections need to identify positive experiences and attributes as a base for self-worth.

The Adult Child movement seldom mentions concepts such as pride, hardiness, resiliency, challenges, and opportunities. These will be discussed in detail in the following chapters. This chapter focuses on accepting the reality and complexity of childhood. We want you to face the pain, abuse, trauma, and deficits in a realistic manner—neither denying nor engaging in self-pity. Examine attitudes, behavior, and feelings about abusive experiences. Identify positive attitudes, behavior, and feelings, whether experienced with parents, relatives, parent surrogates, teachers, neighbors, friends, families, social workers, coaches, or ministers. The key to coming to grips with an abusive or dysfunctional childhood is to develop the motivation, insight, and resources to better manage your adult life and relationships. Life is meant to be lived in the present with anticipation of the future, not controlled by deficits or guilt from the past. Childhood experiences that weigh heavily on self-esteem must be confronted and dealt with so you can lead a responsible, satisfying life.

Growing up in a home where parents were so caught up in their problems and struggles that they neglected the children leaves a legacy of vulnerabilities and deficiencies. Children deserve to have shelter, food, health, and education. Just as important is a consistent, predictable, emotionally nurturing family. When that didn't happen or was inconsistent, the adult faces the challenge of overcoming deficits.

It is important to recognize and talk about neglectful experiences. What coping strategies did you use to deal with neglect or abuse? Which were productive and which destructive? If you stop at this level of awareness, however, you'll feel revictimized. This happens to many in the Adult Child movement. It is psychologically healthy to confront abuse and vulnerabilities, but makes no sense to identify yourself in the victim role or celebrate deficits. The motivation to confront childhood victimization is to progress as an adult, not continue the pattern of neglect or abuse.

You were a victim as a child; you needn't be a victim as an adult. You can learn to act in your best interests and commit time and psychological resources to remedy personal deficiencies. The psychological message of neglect is that you are not worthy or deserving of attention. The message of psychological well-being is that you are a worthwhile, deserving person. Pride grows when the person learns to take care of herself and be a consistent, nurturing parent.

Those who grew up in chaotic, alcoholic homes have painful stories about disrupted birthdays, Thanksgivings, and Christmases that started happily but ended in alcohol-driven fights. Unpredictability is one of the most damaging childhood experiences. Not being able to anticipate an event because it could become explosive and destructive is sad. Children have a right to expect predictable, satisfying family rituals like birthday parties and Christmas dinners. Painful, traumatic memories need to be discussed. The crucial healing experiences involve adult birthdays and holiday dinners that are satisfying. Establishing family rituals for your children is particularly rewarding.

Exercise—Confronting the Guilt and Shame of Childhood

In previous chapters you have engaged (through writing or discussing) in specific exercises to identify childhood abuse and trauma. This exercise is analytic and thematic. It asks you to focus specifically on the deficits of growing up and determining how to cope as an adult.

Begin by listing at least three and a maximum of ten negative experiences from childhood. Be as specific as possible. Examples include guilt you did not save your younger sister from being sexually abused by Stepfather, loss of friends because your family moved so often, phobias and general anxiety caused by unpredictability of parental violence, feeling caught between warring parents where you were forced to take sides, guilt over revealing (or not revealing) family secrets, fear that anger could turn to violence, feeling stigmatized because you were sexually abused by an uncle, lack of respect for family relationships, being caught in the middle of court proceedings, lack of trust in social work and mental health services that let you down, adolescent use of alcohol or drugs to escape the pain of a dysfunctional family, dropping out of school and not attaining vocational skills, being impulsive and not learning to delay gratification.

As you examine this list, see it as a confrontation with the shame and guilt caused by abusive incidents. Next to each negative experience write what you need to do to effectively cope with these deficits and traumas. For example, ask parent or sibling for information so you have a clearer perspective on the incident, write a letter to the perpetrator (that you choose not to mail) expressing hurt and anger, join a self-help group, read two books on this type of abuse to reduce stigma, establish holiday rituals for your family of creation that are predictable and satisfying, consult a minister or therapist to reduce guilt, take night school classes to learn academic or practical skills you missed growing up, take a class in communication, assertiveness, or parenting skills, request an apology from a parent, enlist the help of your spouse or best friend to insure you will not repeat abusive patterns in your life. These coping techniques are not meant to rid you of all bad feelings, but to make the feelings and traumas of the past less powerful. The "demons" of childhood abuse cannot be allowed to dominate your life and self-esteem. Crucial to this exercise is the realistic understanding you have vulnerabilities and deficits but these are changeable and manageable. You did survive—you need not be an adult victim.

Exercise—Identifying Positive Coping Techniques
and Strengths from Childhood

You owe yourself this exercise, not just to put your childhood in perspective, but to recognize and take pride in coping techniques and resiliency. We suggest creating two lists—one about positive coping in childhood and the second on how these and other techniques promote adult functioning. This exercise is best done with friends, siblings, and/or a spouse. This is not just compensating for abuse, but recognizing strengths which have inherent value. Examples of childhood coping and strengths include developing social, academic, or athletic skills, learning to listen to and support siblings, using artistic creativity to express feelings, keeping a diary to provide a thoughtful perspective, starting work at fourteen and managing your money, choosing friends with supportive families and building strong bonds, having a special relationship with grandparents, learning to cook and take care of yourself, becoming a leader of a church youth group. Examples of adult coping techniques and strengths include being able to respond empathically to the pain of others, having an intuition about dangerous people and situations, recognizing negative experiences from childhood which serve as a base that keep difficult life experiences in perspective, taking pride in adult accomplishments, committing to a more successful life and marriage than your parents, having confidence in your ability to cope with difficult life situations, forming closer bonds with siblings, friends, or other families, and taking pride in being a resilient and hardy adult. As you share your list, be open to feedback and additions. This exercise is not to minimize childhood abuse, but to recognize and acknowledge strengths and coping skills.

THE SPOUSE AS SUPPORTER, NOT CRITIC

The spouse is the one most likely to hear childhood stories and traumas. Disclosing personal pain and vulnerabilities assumes he will respond in an empathic, supportive manner.

Using sensitive information as a weapon during a fight is a betrayal of trust and can cause revictimization. This is the worst type of dirty fighting, and results in an alienated marriage. One advantage of an intimate relationship (whether spouse, best friend, therapist, mentor, grandparent) is trust enough to reveal sad or painful experiences that will be understood and supported. Being listened to in a respectful, caring way is a special, powerful validation. Your spouse is an intimate friend who will empathize and not turn vulnerabilities against you. It helps you regain the intimacy and security denied by an abusive childhood. The greater the self-disclosure, the more vulnerable the person makes herself. That is why it is so devastating if trust is broken and the couple engage in dirty fighting. When sharing intimate feelings and experiences with a spouse, best friend, sibling, or mentor carefully assess the person's trustworthiness. An intimate marriage and/or quality friendship(s) promotes self-esteem. Choose well and take the risk to share pain, vulnerabilities, deficits, as well as strengths and joy.

Jill and Nathan. Jill and Nathan met at a mutual friend's Super Bowl party. Jill at twenty-four and Nathan at twenty-five were wearying of the singles scene. Both had vowed to themselves not to repeat the trap of adult children from dysfunctional families and marry young to get the love and self-esteem they lacked in childhood. Nathan had been in three relationships—each lasted over a year—but never seriously considered marriage. Jill had two marriage offers, but could not envision sharing her life with either man.

Jill was attracted by Nathan's interest in people. He enjoyed sports, but was not the crazy jock so many males at the party seemed to be. Jill had learned not to trust her initial attraction, but to get to know the man before deciding if romantic interest was a possibility. Nathan made a rapid assessment of his attraction. He had enough female "buddies;" Nathan wanted an emotional/romantic relationship with Jill.

They enjoyed the football game, especially since their team

won. As the victory party became rowdier, Nathan asked Jill if she wanted to go for coffee and dessert. Talking in a quiet booth is a good way to get to know someone. They discovered they belonged to different volleyball leagues and hiking groups. Nathan enjoyed jazz while Jill preferred opera, but both were open to trying something new. They both enjoyed bike riding and made a date to go on a twenty-five-mile ride the following Saturday.

They did not discuss family background until the third date. Nathan came from a difficult family who lived two hundred miles away. He had purposely moved from his home town because he wanted to put distance between him and his family. Nathan had never introduced any of his woman friends to the family. Jill's family was scattered all over. Jill was close to Mother, who had met two of the men Jill had been involved with. Jill was forthcoming about the effects of her mother's two failed marriages and stepfamily relationships on her own sense of well-being. These experiences convinced Jill of the importance of establishing a viable, stable marriage before having children. Nathan was used to hearing women (especially those in Adult Children recovery groups) complain endlessly about childhood, parents, and dysfunctional patterns. Although he listened, he minimally self-disclosed and did not find that these conversations enhanced relationships. He was impressed that Jill was not whiny, but shared information, perceptions, and experiences. This served as an invitation for Nathan. He worried ''heavy'' subjects would spoil the romantic glow, but as the relationship evolved, he realized Jill was right—self-disclosure increased emotional intimacy.

After four months, theirs was becoming a serious relationship. Jill resolved she would not marry unless she was sure of the man's commitment and there would be no surprises. This included knowing about his family and his knowing about hers. Jill was an amateur photographer and kept scrapbooks of photos of significant people and events. She knew the relationship with Nathan was serious when she put photos of him in one of her scrapbooks. Jill asked Nathan if he was interested in seeing the photos and hearing about her experiences. Nathan was, but said don't expect me to reciprocate immediately. Jill assured him she didn't need to do things "tit for tat."

Jill's father left Mother two months before Jill was born. He sent birthday cards and saw her three times when she was very young, but Jill had no memories of him. Mother was bitter, feeling abandoned emotionally and financially. Jill was cared for by grandparents. Her first memories, at ages three and four, involved being with Mother at the grandparents and playing with cousins. When Jill was five Mother married an army sergeant major with two older sons. They divorced when Jill was eleven, but she remembers those six years as the worst in her life. Chaos and unpredictability were pervasive in this blended family. There were three moves, ongoing fights between Mother and Stepfather, drinking and rages where he would hit Mother and the sons (although not Jill). The stepbrothers were mean and Jill remembers two incidents where the younger one masturbated against her. There was one daughter, Joanna, born from Mother's second marriage. Jill was a caretaker for Joanna because Mother's life was in a state of constant stress and disruption. Joanna ran away from home at fifteen, was arrested at eighteen for shoplifting, and is serving a five-year sentence for transporting stolen goods. Jill urged Joanna to obtain a G.E.D. degree while in jail. Jill keeps contact with her twenty-one-year-old sister and hasn't given up on her, but realizes she can't rescue Joanna from herself.

Mother was fifty-two, a restaurant manager who shared a rental house with two women. Mother's psychological flaw was that she'd centered her life around a man to make her feel worthwhile. She'd had two awful marriages, and felt stigmatized and embarrassed by the divorces. She was an attractive and socially active woman, but Jill was unimpressed with the men she dated. Jill loved Mother, but was committed to living her life differently.

As Nathan looked at pictures and heard stories, his respect for Jill increased. She didn't deny the past, but didn't whine or feel sorry for herself. The one time she cried was when Jill showed pictures of Joanna as a child. Nathan was both impressed and worried about Jill's determination to have a healthy marriage and family. Nathan wondered whether he could share her dreams and life.

A month later, Jill invited Nathan for a weekend trip to visit Mother. It was a beautiful day for a drive, but there was a silent tension hanging over them. Halfway there, Nathan asked her to pull off the road and accompany him on a short hike. They walked twenty minutes and found a rocky area with a pretty view. Jill was surprised by Nathan's passionate kiss and tender touching. They had been a sexual couple for over three months and Jill liked the fact that Nathan was a caring, yet passionate, lover. She was confused about the source of the passion now. As they walked back to the car, Jill mentioned this in a joking way and Nathan said when he was tense or unsure he turned to sex as a coping mechanism. He assured Jill this was not a problem, but realized how uptight he was about the visit. Jill reassured him he didn't have to impress Mother, that this wasn't a test.

Nathan found the weekend different than expected. There was an easy relationship between Jill and Mother, and he heard stories about Jill's childhood. Jill was a better-educated, more successful person than Mother, but this did not disrupt their emotional bond. Both Mother's and Jill's eyes filled with tears when talking about Joanna. Jill wrote her sister weekly and visited at least five times a year. Jill was not ashamed of her family or childhood, but realized that the history of violence, sexual abuse, parental alcoholism, unsuccessful relationships, and chaos left her with deficits and vulnerabilities. She worried that her personal and family goals were unrealistic. As they drove home, Nathan listened carefully. He said her plans and goals made sense and that she deserved to succeed. The more they talked, the more Nathan respected and felt close to Jill.

Two months later, Nathan asked Jill to marry him. Jill was thrilled and receptive, but the realistic part of her insisted that first she needed to understand him, his family, and life experiences. Nathan was irritated and they had an argument. Jill loved Nathan and wanted to marry him. She trusted his intentions and knew he was a good person, but insisted they talk out issues about a life together, including vulnerabilities from the past. Nathan could be stubborn—he agreed to talk about hard issues of careers and money, contraception and children, where they would live, how to organize their lives, friendships, a commitment to not have affairs, and how they would problem solve and manage conflict. Both were surprised how well these conversations went and how many values and goals they shared. Still, Jill insisted on meeting Nathan's family and understanding his vulnerabilities.

Nathan arranged an early Sunday dinner at his parents' home. During the three-hour drive, Nathan talked a great deal about career plans—sharing fears and hopes. Jill did not know what to expect from this visit, but was surprised to find an attractive middle-class home, a cordial greeting from his parents, and a spectacularly presented meal. The conversation about careers, public affairs, and economic topics was lively and interesting. Father seemed sophisticated and well-spoken and Mother, although more reserved, was fine.

It was not until the end of the meal that Jill realized there had been no talk of family, no family stories, and no personal questions asked of her. Jill noticed there were no family pictures. She knew Nathan had an older brother and sister, but no one mentioned them. When Jill made a comment about wishing she'd had an older sibling the conversation stopped. Father became very red in the face and Mother was so upset she couldn't speak. Nathan shot a cold, cutting glance at Jill and began a long, convoluted story which refocused the conversation on a nonsensitive topic. The tone was light and cordial for another hour before they left for the long drive home. Jill got a hug from Mother and a handshake from Father, although there was no touching between Nathan and his parents.

In the car, Nathan was animated and affectionate. He was obviously relieved that the ordeal was over and had gone better than expected. His parents were really taken by Jill. She was pleased, but commented that there were obviously sensitive issues and secrets which she trusted Nathan would eventually share. Nathan was quiet for a few minutes and then said his brother was a recruiter for Jews for Jesus and his sister had

joined a Hasidic group and lived in Brooklyn. Nathan's pater-
nal grandparents had come from Germany before the Holocaust
and his maternal grandparents were Russian Jews. Conflict
over heritage and religion had torn his family apart, and Nathan
wanted no part of it. He joked he was a "committed agnostic."

Religious belief had played a minor role in Jill's life. She
was baptized in a Presbyterian church and Stepfather had been
a Lutheran. Jill believed in God, but found organized religion
hypocritical, and resented that it had not helped her mother or
sister. Jill realized religion had not been mentioned in their
discussions of couple issues. Jill wanted her children to be
aware of their ethnic heritages and not be ashamed of or deny
them. She wanted them to attend Sunday school, but didn't
want them raised with a narrow-minded or guilt-inducing view
of God and religious orthodoxy.

Jill asked Nathan about the legacy of religious and ethnic
conflict and secretiveness in his family. He said he'd never
confronted it in those terms. Nathan realized there had been a
great deal of tension and alienation in the family. Religious
and ethnic issues weren't spoken about, much less worked
through. This resulted in a fragmented family with siblings
who were zealots. To be a successful couple, Jill and Nathan
would have to talk out issues and not allow secrets. Silence
and secrets can split a family. Nathan vowed that would not
happen in his marriage and family.

Three days later, Nathan invited Jill to attend an adult education course on the Holocaust. If his children were to appreciate
their Jewish heritage, he and his future wife would need greater
understanding. Nathan had no desire to make the Holocaust a
dominant theme, but did want to increase awareness and be
able to talk, not as a zealot, but with pride about his cultural
heritage. Jill wanted to be knowledgeable about Judaism so
she could convey that to their children.

Jill and Nathan talked about their families of origin in a
sharing, respectful manner, not in a put-down "damaged
goods" way. They realized there were significant areas of
deficit and vulnerability. The spouse reinforces strengths and
helps monitor traps. Jill did not ask Nathan to be perfect or for

them to have an ideal family, but to be a respectful, trusting, and intimate spouse and father. Talking and sharing was a challenge Nathan felt ready for. He was realistic, and no longer the cynic, about marriage and family.

A PERSONAL NOTE

Emily and I met in spring 1966 at Southern Illinois University. In August, we drove to a small town near Peoria, to meet Emily's family and then to Chicago to meet mine. The weekend we visited near Peoria there was a large family reunion. While growing up, Emily felt a good deal of family love and support, although she realized her parents' marriage was dysfunctional with hostility punctured by outbursts of violence. Disrespect and spousal violence were also pervasive in her extended family.

I was the first man she'd brought home. The family was wary of this Chicago boy who was a graduate student in psychology and looked at life in a way they didn't understand. Emily had a special role in her family—she was the first to attend college. They worried this new man would undermine her life. I enjoyed meeting my soon-to-be relatives, but was aware that I wanted a life, marriage, and family quite different from theirs. On the three-hour drive to Chicago, I told Emily I was impressed by how she related to her family and had adopted positive traits while staying away from the traps. Emily said if our marriage was to succeed, we should not live in Illinois. We needed space for our lives, marriage, and family to thrive. I had not considered this, but agreed to think and talk about it.

The three-day visit to Chicago crystallized our thinking. Em's family could be loud and combative, while mine appeared quiet on the surface and then would unpredictably erupt like a volcano. The first night at two A.M., there was an explosive argument about my younger sister's drinking.

The next day Mother talked of my idyllic childhood and produced family photos. What the photos couldn't show was a dysfunctional family with a poor marriage, an unpredictably angry father who ruled through violence and threats of violence, an insecure, physically ill mother filled with secrets and conflicts, and a son and daughter who were not close and experienced problems and concerns they couldn't verbalize. By the time I was ten, I realized my family was strange and I purposely began to establish relationships with friends and academic mentors to provide support and guidance. School until fourth grade was a disaster, although it got better by eighth grade. Academically and socially, high school was a marked improvement. I was a late bloomer who blossomed in college. At twenty-three, in graduate school and engaged to Emily, I had self-esteem, felt like a survivor, and was looking forward to marriage and family.

As Emily and I drove back to southern Illinois, we asked each other whether we were still committed to marriage. I observed that at least there were no secrets. Emily said she loved and respected me, but needed to trust that I was committed to a marriage unlike that of either of our parents. We would have to think more, talk more, and plan in order not to repeat the negative patterns of our families. We would need to trust each other and not be each other's worst critic.

It has been a struggle, not without difficulties and mistakes, but we take pride in our marriage. There is a solid base of respect and trust, and there has been no violence. We did a better job parenting our children than our parents did and hope our children will do even better with their families. We hope and plan to be active grandparents.

FROM A DYSFUNCTIONAL FAMILY TO A FUNCTIONAL LIFE AND FAMILY OF CREATION

The principal reasons to confront the abuse and victimization of childhood are to promote adult functioning and allow the person to be a survivor who can build a satisfying life and cohesive family. You were a victim as a child—you deserve to be a survivor as an adult. These chapters and exercises have helped you confront abuse and trauma, acknowledge you are a survivor, and identify strengths and coping techniques which serve you well. Be aware of traps so you don't repeat destructive patterns. Be committed to a satisfying life and healthy, functional family of creation. Is it that simple? No, it's not simple and success is not guaranteed. It is worthwhile and deserves the time and psychological energy. For the sake of those you care about—friends, spouse, children, relatives—it is in your best interest to think, feel, and be a survivor.

Good intentions are not enough: life is not a series of New Year's resolutions. You need a commitment to change, a plan of change. Utilize resources (including self-help groups and professional therapy) which facilitate the change process, promote the discipline to implement a change program, provide a back-up plan if you get off track or hit a roadblock, and a system to maintain changes. The key for maintaining motivation is that you deserve to lead a more functional life than your family of origin and develop relationships (marriage, parenting, friendships) that are nurturing and satisfying. Growing up in a dysfunctional family leaves deficits and vulnerabilities which must be addressed, not denied or viewed with shame. It also leaves you with strengths and a commitment to meeting the challenges of a functional, loving, and satisfying life.

II
PRESENT AND FUTURE

9
THE VICTIM CYCLE

Am I a victim or a survivor? How can I live my life in the present when my past was a personal holocaust? My family was crazy and this caused my present problems. Until I get to the heart of the pain—really grieve for my wounded child—can I ever be healthy? Through years of therapy, self-help groups, and journaling, I have vague memories of sexual abuse. How can I know if it's true? My uncle says my mother was crazy and subjected me to weird rituals. Should I believe him? For the past five years I've presented speeches and written articles about my incest experiences. People treat me like a guru, so why do I feel like a fraud? How do I know I've gotten all the pain out? My group tells me I'm in denial. Are they right? If I forgive my parents, does it enable them to deny the family dysfunction? My spouse and friends say they're tired of hearing my stories of abuse. Are they trying to invalidate me? I believe what happened to me is unforgivable and unforgettable. Will I always be controlled by it? Since I'm the victim of an alcoholic family and incest, can I ever attain psychological well-being?

These and other questions pervade the Adult Child movement. Is it true that it takes years of self-help groups and therapy to deal with the pain and shame of abuse? Do you ever

127

resolve it or are you always (at least in part) a victim? The first section of this book explored issues dealing with abuse and victimization in the past. This section will focus on confronting the victim role in the present. A real danger is the victim/low self-esteem trap, which makes the person vulnerable to being revictimized. As a child, you did not have the awareness or resources to prevent victimization. As an adult you do—you can learn to think, feel, and act like a survivor. You deserve to be a survivor, not feel like a victim or play out the victim role.

THE VICTIM CYCLE

There are three levels of victimization. The first involves the actual abusive incidents—whether physical abuse, sexual abuse, witnessing violence, parents engaging in out-of-control drinking or drug abuse, neglect, or chaos. The second level of victimization is how you reacted as a child to the incidents. One extreme is to deny them and keep them a secret. The danger is that the secrets become more powerful and distorted with time. You feel ashamed and stigmatized and mistakenly believe if anyone knew they would treat you like ''damaged goods'' and reject you. The opposite extreme is to reveal the incidents indiscriminately and feel victimized by people's reactions. You feel guilty, blamed, embarrassed, and/or labeled. Typically the child wants three things: 1) to understand the incidents, 2) not to feel blamed or guilty, and 3) the incidents to stop and the family to function better. Instead, confusion, blaming, guilt, and wishing it would disappear predominate. Rather than trauma being dealt with in a helpful and supportive way, the child's life and self-esteem is defined by abuse and victimization. The third level is the adult's self-concept as a victim. Abuse and trauma controls the person's past and present life. In response to the question ''Who are you?'' the answer is ''I'm an adult child of alcoholics,'' ''I'm a victim of incest,'' ''I grew up in a dysfunctional family,'' ''I'm co-dependent.'' Childhood abuse is elevated to the controlling definition of the person's life. The third level of victimization (partially self-inflicted) is as bad, if not worse, than child abuse. Victimization becomes a self-fulfilling prophecy.

THE SURVIVOR CYCLE

Life is meant to be lived in the present with planning for the future, not controlled by trauma of the past. The survivor believes "Living well is the best revenge." The survivor deserves to have and is committed to living a successful, loving life.

At the first level, the adult survivor is able to explore the complex experience of growing up. The abusive, dysfunctional, and traumatic experiences are carefully assessed and dealt with. Vulnerabilities and deficits are confronted, not denied or minimized. These are regarded as traps to be aware of and monitored so they don't subvert adult life. Personal strengths, compensations, and coping techniques are recognized and reinforced.

At the second level of surviving, the person does not blame herself for the abuse or feel guilty. Responsibility for abuse lies with the perpetrator, not the child. Although it would be ideal if abuse had been therapeutically dealt with at the time, the person acknowledges she did the best she could with available understandings and resources, and did survive. Children want to understand abusive incidents in the least pejorative manner and to have a well-functioning, non-abusive family. Children deserve to grow up in a nurturing, supportive, secure environment. If that is not possible, they search out nurturance and support from other sources. As an adult, the child thinks about the past in an aware, realistic manner, realizing it cannot be changed and is neither ashamed of nor obsessed by it. She shares stories in a discriminating manner and asks for help from people and groups she respects and trusts have her best interests in mind.

The third level is the most important. Adopting an adult self-concept as a survivor who deserves a functional life, healthy relationships, and successful family of creation is crucial. You did survive and can thrive, not be a sad or angry person who views himself as a damaged victim. You can learn to take care of yourself and act in your best interests. This does not mean being selfish at the expense of others. Your best interest includes forming healthy, mutually supportive relationships. Self-recrimination, self-pity, or abusive relationships are antithetical to being a survivor. Accepting the challenge to succeed and taking pride in coping skills is integral. He confronts and deals with past abuse with awareness of traps and vulnerabilities. However, he keeps the focus where it belongs—in the present—and takes responsibility, not feeling controlled by the past.

AWARENESS OF THE VICTIM/SURVIVOR PROCESS

Being aware of the victim/survivor cycle is a necessary first step, but it has to be followed by cognitive, behavioral, and emotional skills of taking care of yourself and acting as a survivor. Awareness of self-defeating patterns and psychological traps is necessary, but the crucial step is committing to and implementing healthy attitudes and behavior. It isn't as simple as using "willpower" or "positive thinking." The best way to avoid falling into traps is to have a clear, specific plan to engage in a healthy alternative. Awareness of the self-defeating nature of the victimization cycle is a start, but the survivor has to develop a lifeview that facilitates psychological well-being.

Attitudes, behavior, and emotional expression which are congruent serve her well. When disappointed or defeated, rather than blaming the past or engaging in self-pity, she takes a problem-solving approach. Is this a problem that can be overcome or does it have to be accepted? If the latter, be sure it does not reinforce feelings of victimization or low self-esteem. One trap of the Adult Child movement is to interpret every personal problem or life defeat as a result of childhood abuse. Behavior is multicausal and multidimensional. Most problems cannot be perfectly resolved (no matter what self-help books or groups promise), but can be significantly reduced or altered. Personal responsibility and self-confidence motivate the survivor to address issues and successfully problem solve. Being assertive, analyzing and weighing alternatives and developing agreements and action plans are part of the repertoire of survivors.

Contrary to media myths, growing up in an abusive home does not mean you are destined to repeat that pattern. Most people who grow up in an alcoholic family, for example, do not become alcoholic or engage in addictive behavior. People from abusive backgrounds, however, are *prone* to repeat dysfunctional patterns, so they need to monitor traps and commit to a healthy, functional life. An optimistic approach to life is part of psychological well-being.

If there was incest in the family of origin, it does not mean there will be incest in the family of creation. However, sexuality is likely to be a difficult, sensitive area so the adult needs to use educational and therapeutic resources to develop a healthy approach to sexuality. Knowledge is power. The worst trap is to repeat incest in the family of creation. This is a greater risk for males, since men are much more likely to be perpetrators. A man who was the victim of incest needs to gain comfort and awareness in his sexuality so that it enhances his life and intimate relationship.

People who grew up in neglectful or chaotic families are at risk to repeat that pattern in their marriages and families. If you lack a positive model of an intimate relationship or parenting, it's harder to incorporate these attitudes and skills into your present life. Often the person sets an unrealistic expectation of an all-loving marriage or a perfectly nurturing family, and when he runs into normal problems, he gives up in despair and becomes inconsistent or neglectful. It is healthier to set the goal to be a "good enough" parent—consistent, nurturing, and open to feedback.

Developing and maintaining psychological well-being, an intimate marriage, and a nurturing family is not an easy task. It takes awareness and commitment, as well as the ability to deal with difficulties while utilizing communication and problem-solving skills. Even when life is difficult and discouraging, engaging in abusive or destructive behavior is not acceptable. You resolve nothing by drinking, drugging, sexually abusing, physically abusing, or hurting yourself. One of our favorite AA sayings is "Nothing is so bad that getting drunk can't make it worse." A core element of personal pride is that you don't harm anyone and are committed to breaking the cycle of abuse and dysfunction. If you find yourself engaging in behavior that victimizes others, confront the problem. You'll need professional therapy to break the pattern. Rather than viewing this as a failure, admitting you need help in overcoming an abusive or addictive behavior is a sign of strength.

Exercise—Confronting the Victim Role and Being a Survivor

This is not an exercise to be done alone. Share this with spouse, friends, or siblings. The focus is strengthening the commitment to being an adult survivor. This includes being aware of deficits and vulnerabilities from the past and having a specific method of monitoring and intervening (often with the help of a spouse, close friend, therapist, or self-help group) so you don't fall into traps and act out self-defeating behavior. Examples of such behavior include becoming anxious and phobic when under stress, reacting to negative feedback by personalizing and catastrophizing, anger quickly accelerating as if confronting a life-and-death situation, feeling inhibited or numb during sex, feeling it's a personal attack when a child is misbehaving or angry, during a verbal argument, feeling overwhelmed by the irrational fear it will degenerate into violence, having a powerful, automatic reaction of defensiveness or anger when anything goes wrong, obsessing how unfair life is, envying people who came from healthier families, when adult siblings have trouble, recalling feelings of family dysfunction, feeling overwhelmed by a sense of unfairness at having to take care of an ailing parent who abused you, fearing Father will abuse your child, being frustrated when you repeat dysfunctional parenting patterns, drinking as a way of dealing with stress or depression. Once you've identified traps, design an appropriate monitoring and intervention system for each. Good intentions and willpower are not enough—you need a specific plan, including utilizing the support and reinforcement of others.

Examples of monitoring and intervention systems include:

1. You start to lose your temper with your four-year-old because he won't get his coat on and fear you might hit instead of giving three spanks. Ask your spouse to temporarily take over the parenting task. Don't put yourself down as an "abusive parent," but do talk with spouse and other parents about techniques so that getting the child dressed in the morning is less stressful. Make a commitment that your anger will not override the child's needs. Either there will be no physical discipline or it will be limited to a maximum of three spanks on the buttocks with an open hand.

2. Dealing with discouragement. If the goal is to be perfectly happy and at peace, you will always feel insecure and inadequate. When people become discouraged, the usual advice is to go into deeper therapy, attend more 12-step meetings, get at the primal pain of the inner child. For most people, that's the wrong intervention. You can be healthier, more competent, with higher self-esteem, but the truth of the human condition is you will not be perfect, totally at peace, or self-actualized. Set goals (with the help of others—friends, spouse, therapist, minister) that are meaningful and which you have a good chance of reaching. When you fail or are discouraged, consider three alternatives: 1) You can succeed at this; refocus and use a new approach and new resources. 2) It's normal to fail; lower your goals or consider it a slip and time will alleviate the problem. 3) Admit in this area you have failed, but it doesn't mean you are a failure as a person. Learn from the experience and focus on something more reinforcing. Play to your strengths; don't define yourself by failures and deficits.

3. You revert to compulsive behavior when under stress, apologize profusely, and feel guilty. Confront the self-defeating cycle of inappropriate behavior/guilt/low self-esteem. Positive motivation promotes change; guilt and beating up on yourself keeps you in the same rut. Choose a

therapist, group, or friends who support a positive change process. Change involves triumphs and setbacks; it is never perfect. It is crucial to confront and reduce compulsive, self-defeating behavior.

4. Trying to rescue siblings or parents. Your prime commitment is to yourself, marriage, and children. If you don't take care of yourself, you will be of no help to others. The suggested coping technique is to talk with the sibling or parent when there is not the pressure of a crisis. Establish realistic parameters for help you can and cannot give. The guideline is "Don't make promises you can't keep." Carefully consider the time, financial, emotional, and practical help you can give. People respond in acute crises, but cannot maintain that level of help when problems become chronic or it's the fifth crisis in a year. Focus on support in the present, not making up for the past. Guilt or compensation is not a healthy motivation. Encourage the sibling or parent to take responsibility for his life and set realistic goals. You can be helpful and supportive, but cannot rescue or take control of his life.

As you review your lists of traps and coping strategies, realize that these will change over time and with circumstances. Monitoring traps so you don't fall into the victim role is the easiest part of the process. Leading your life as a survivor is a challenge that requires awareness, realistic plans and goals, adaptability, and judgment. Coping with setbacks and difficulties, resiliency, ability to refocus, and commitment to leading a functional, loving life are worthwhile challenges.

THE WORST TRAP—VICTIMIZING OTHERS

Only a minority of people from abusive backgrounds abuse others. However, when this does happen, it's harmful to all concerned. Being a perpetrator is not the way to deal with victimization. Repeating the past and victimizing others is the worst form of revictimization. You not only lose respect for yourself but perpetuate the cycle of abuse and trauma by creating new victims.

Victimizing others physically and sexually is a particular trap for males. As an abused person the man feels powerless and deficient. As an inappropriate and harmful way to regain power, he dominates and uses others. The anger that welled up when the boy was physically beaten by his father is acted out twenty years later when he beats his son. It is not to discipline the child, but to express anger. In good parenting, the emotional needs of the child come before the emotional needs of the parent. In an abusive relationship the adult's needs, whether anger expression or sexual arousal, are acted out in harmful ways at the expense of the child's best interest. Halting the pattern of abuse is a source of personal pride. Continuing the abusive pattern is a personal revictimization, victimizing others and feeding the abusive cycle.

If the harsh reality is that you are engaged in abusing others, what should you do? It is almost impossible to break this cycle on your own. You have to confront the compulsive, abusive behavior and be committed to eliminating it. Moderation is the goal of most human behavior, but for abusive behavior it is to abstain and break the pattern. You need to learn a new set of attitudes, behavior, and emotional responses. This requires individual, couple, family, and/or group psychotherapy. It might mean involvement with a 12-step program or other form of self-help group. The road to eliminating compulsive, addictive behavior is seldom easy. A key concept is to learn from lapses and not allow a lapse to become a relapse. It is crucial to not become discouraged and give up. Abusive behavior not only revictimizes you, it hurts others. The commitment to a life free of abuse and victimization is paramount. Guilt and shame reinforce abusive behavior. Pride in addressing the problem and utilizing all your resources to promote change is the path to eliminating self-defeating behavior.

Rick and Stephanie. Forty-seven-year-old Rick has been married to forty-two-year-old Stephanie for four years. They provide a good example of the difficult process of change from a victim to a survivor. This was Rick's third marriage and Stephanie's second. They were committed to this being a successful, secure marriage. They wanted a blended family free of abuse so all members could grow and thrive in a healthy, nurturing environment.

Rick grew up in a depressed family. When Rick was eight his oldest brother, age twelve, was killed in a tragic athletic accident. His parents never grieved the loss. Rick and his younger brother recall growing up "under a dark cloud." The parents stayed married, but it was a means of mutual torture. Mother blamed Father because he'd promoted athletics. Rick and his brother were not allowed to participate in sports, which made them feel isolated, shunned by peers. Father stopped parenting and became an alienated, angry alcoholic. When Rick was eighteen, his father died in a single-car accident while driving when drunk.

While growing up, Rick attempted to be the good boy who would cheer Mother and cure her depression. He failed. To escape this oppressive family, Rick joined the Navy at nineteen, married at twenty, had a child at twenty-one, and was divorced at twenty-two. Rick is now a grandfather of two. Even through bad times, Rick made child-support payments and had a special relationship with his daughter. It helped that his first wife had a successful second marriage and they were able to maintain a cordial relationship.

Rick's second marriage was more destructive than his first—the only saving grace was that there were no children. Rick and his second wife met at a bar—two lonely people looking to be rescued. The result was the opposite—they dragged each other into a three-year battle of drugs, alcohol, spouse abuse, and crises. During this time, Rick's younger brother declared he was gay and left for California. Mother was hospitalized for severe depression and discharged to a nursing home where she died five years later. When he thought of his parents, Rick was not angry or blaming, but sad for their inability to deal with the loss of their son and the resulting loss of their lives.

The sadder Rick felt, the needier he felt, and the angrier his wife became. Their fights grew more volatile and threatening. Finally, the wife's family came to get her and warned him not to contact her. At first Rick was enraged, but realized the only way to break the destructive cycle was total disengagement. The divorce process was a complex legal labyrinth which extended over two years. Not having contact with his ex-wife made it bearable.

After this divorce, Rick vowed to not marry again. He remained involved with his daughter and became successful in his career. Rick remembers these as good years. It was not until Stephanie came into his life that he even considered remarriage.

Stephanie had three sons from her first marriage. Stephanie's family of origin swung from religious orthodoxy and 12-step adherence to chaos and unpredictability. Father was a rags to riches and back to rags salesman, while Mother was a born-again Christian who fought like a Roman gladiator. Stephanie felt like a military brat because she moved so often—attending three different high schools. Her goal was to marry and establish a stable life. As often happens when people go from one extreme to another, Stephanie overshot her goal. What she took as stability and serenity was a severely depressed husband. He worked as a factory foreman, but lost this job after fifteen years because he was psychiatrically hospitalized for the third time in five years.

Stephanie was both mother and father to her sons. The husband was so depressed he had no energy to be a spouse or parent. The healthiest thing Stephanie did was to build a support network around school, church, Boy Scouts, and athletic teams. Separating after eighteen years of marriage was very sad. She realized she could not maintain herself and family while taking care of her husband. He was placed in a church-based residential home for handicapped people and functioned as a maintenance worker. He sent birthday and holiday cards to the boys, but otherwise did not maintain contact. Stephanie felt bad for her sons. Children, however, are often more aware than we give them credit for. They realized their father was a sad man who had little role in their lives.

Stephanie wanted to remarry, but was wise enough to keep away from married men who suggested affairs and divorced men who were looking for someone to take care of them. Stephanie was impressed by how Rick managed his life, his relationship with his adult daughter, and how well he related to her sons. Rick was a board member of the community athletic association and a basketball coach.

They'd known each other two years before their first semi-date after a season-ending basketball party. Their next date was a hike in the country where they discussed outdoor experiences—they both hated the singles ritual of talking about ex-spouses and telling gruesome life stories. The following day Stephanie took the risk, called Rick, and told him how much she'd enjoyed herself. She then invited him to a professional basketball game. At the end of that date, Rick made the ritual sexual pass. In a nice but firm manner, Stephanie said she had nothing to prove sexually and assumed Rick didn't either, and that for her sex came after, not before, a serious talk.

It was Stephanie who initiated sex three weeks later. This was her way of saying she was attracted and had hope for their relationship. Both Rick and Stephanie looked forward to a sexually satisfying relationship. Stephanie used birth control pills, but insisted Rick use a condom to protect against the HIV virus and other sexually transmitted diseases. Once established as a couple, they went for HIV testing. They tested negative and were pleased to get rid of condoms, which increased sexual enjoyment.

After three months, it was Rick who initiated the painful task of talking about the past. This was out of character, but he'd decided Stephanie was a special person whom he could trust. Rick opened up about his family of origin and fatally flawed marriages. Stephanie was an empathic listener who accepted Rick's stories in a nonjudgmental manner. She decided not to share her stories with him until the following week, but did disclose her desire to remarry. She'd given up on the first marriage, but not on the hope for an intimate, satisfying marital bond. Rick was surprised by the genuineness and spirit of Stephanie's desire. He'd grown used to cynical, defeating talk about relationships and marriage. Rick shared fears about a third failed marriage. She did not dismiss this, but said people couldn't be governed by fears.

Stephanie told the story of growing up and marriage differently than Rick. She did not cover up or minimize the pain, but it was not the dominant theme. She shared what she'd learned about herself and relationships, including pride in coping and succeeding. What most impressed Rick was Stephanie's honesty and not apologizing for her background or life. Stephanie was a proud survivor who looked forward to new challenges—especially an intimate marriage. Stephanie was forthright, but not desperate. Rick did not view women as strong, but Stephanie's strengths and hopes, in addition to her warmth and sexual expressiveness, jarred Rick into considering marriage. Theirs was not a romantic leap of faith, but a well thought-out and talked-out commitment. They were aware of traps from childhood and previous marriages. They pledged to bring out the best in each other and together deal with their blended family.

Being liked and respected as a coach is different from being accepted as a stepfather. Stephanie's sons had never had a real father figure and each was at a different developmental phase. The sixteen-year-old had quite different needs from the ten-year-old. Stephanie helped Rick understand the loyalty the boys felt toward their father. Stephanie did not try to create a stepparent relationship with Rick's young adult daughter, but did develop a "favorite aunt" relationship and formed a special bond with the grandchildren.

Two years into the marriage, Stephanie raised the issue of a baby. She was confident of the marital bond, and wanted a child. As usual, they didn't make an impulsive decision—of all life's choices, a child is the hardest to renege on. When she decided to try to get pregnant three months later, they were immensely pleased to find it was easy. Rick found it strange having a baby who was younger than his grandchildren. The road from being a victim to a survivor can result in some unusual life arrangements. Rick and Stephanie were not concerned with being socially acceptable, but with establishing a life, marriage, and blended family they could be proud of.

TAKING CARE OF YOURSELF AND ACTING IN YOUR BEST INTEREST

An adult child who views himself as a victim and acts out that role cannot blame it on childhood. By his passivity and living in the past he allows life to revictimize him. The core of breaking the victim cycle is to take care of yourself and act in your best interests.

Confront deficits and vulnerabilities from the past. Awareness is power, especially being clear about traps and the commitment not to repeat self-defeating behavior. This requires a change plan and the discipline to implement it. Choosing people who will support, not criticize or nag, is vital. This can be a spouse or close friend, a therapist and/or self-help group. The survivor utilizes all necessary resources to insure life stays on a functional path.

"Acting in your best interests" is such a simple phrase. However, it confronts the stronghold of the victim mentality. Victims are prone to live in the past, procrastinate, and avoid choices and commitments. Their lives are defined by stigma, pain, guilt, and a sense of unfairness. They expect nothing better in the future. The traditional victim was passive, embarrassed, and silent about abuse and the dysfunctional family. With increased publicity, there are more angry victims who speak out and wear the Adult Child label with pride. So much psychological energy goes into anger about the past they don't act in their best interest. It is preferable to be an angry victim than a passive victim. However, both subvert adult life.

You deserve to be a survivor, to conduct your life in a manner where you grow and thrive. An advantage of being an adult is having life choices. Use that responsibility wisely and learn to choose and act in your best interests. This means avoiding traps and making healthy choices. It's important to follow through and successfully implement changes. People from dysfunctional families are used to unrealistic promises and goals, being disappointed and angered by failure. The adult survivor can learn to be responsible for herself, choose well, set realistic goals, develop a change plan, use others as resources and support, and celebrate changes.

CLOSING THOUGHTS

The challenge to an adult who grew up in an abusive or dysfunctional family is to confront the pain, deficits, and vulnerabilities and be a survivor who deserves a satisfying life, intimate relationship, and healthy family of creation. It is crucial to avoid the victim/low self-esteem trap so that you are not vulnerable to being revictimized. Being aware of the self-defeating victim role is important. The survivor deserves to have a healthy life and is determined to learn and utilize cognitive, behavioral, and emotional skills of taking care of herself and acting in her best interest. At a minimum this means monitoring psychological traps and self-defeating patterns so they are not repeated. Optimally, it is establishing a loving, responsible life in which you take pride in overcoming childhood deficits, creating a healthy marriage and family, and perpetuating that pattern for future generations. Take pride parenting your children better than you were parented. Whether a great leap forward or gradual steps, breaking the victim cycle is a source of personal and family pride.

10
CO-DEPENDENCE—AN OVERUSED CONCEPT

"Hi, I'm Mary and I'm co-dependent." This sentence is being said by thousands of people each night at meetings in towns and cities throughout the country. Books on identifying and overcoming co-dependence sell over a million copies a year. Advocates claim 97% of people are co-dependent. Is that possible? What does it mean? The overwhelming majority of people who identify themselves as co-dependent are women. Is co-dependence a sexist label, a symbol of oppression? Is co-dependence a true syndrome or a "pop psychology" phrase which will disappear as quickly as it arose?

The origin of the co-dependence concept was alcoholism treatment. Alcoholism is an addiction, a dependence, that controls the alcoholic's life. The alcoholic's spouse is co-dependent, her life controlled by alcoholism. The children are powerfully affected because they deny the reality of having an alcoholic parent, supress feelings, and do not talk about or acknowledge destructive behavior. "Don't know, don't feel, don't speak." The concept of alcoholism as a family disease was extended to co-dependence. From there, co-dependence was used to define a variety of problems, especially "love addiction"—a person totally dependent on the presence and love of another. Examples of this type of co-dependent relationship could be the mother dependent on being needed and loved by her children, the employee who needs the recognition and approval of his colleagues and boss, the welfare worker dependent on clients' coming to her to rescue them. Most common was the woman who needed a lover or spouse to make her feel worthwhile. Another form of co-dependence was the relationship object or group—money, religion, a house, gambling, work, sex, a political ideology, sports, a hobby, and even 12-step recovery groups. The concept of co-dependence has become so broad and vague as to be virtually meaningless.

People are neither meant to be isolated and alienated nor to become so dependent on another person, group, or ideology that they can't function independently. As is true of most aspects of psychological well-being, being at either extreme is unhealthy. Maintaining a sense of balance and having multiple sources of self-esteem are the antidotes to co-dependence. The either-or question "Am I an addict" is not relevant to the dimension of independence/dependence. It is a continuum, not a dichotomy. The extreme of the person who lives an isolated, alienated life (as articulated in the classic Simon and Garfunkel song, "I am a rock, I am an island") subverts psychological well-being. The other extreme of a symbiotic attachment to a person where you feel unable to function without him is self-negating. Each individual has worth, dignity, and integrity. People need others to give their lives a sense of meaning, connection, and continuity. The key is maintaining a balance between self and others.

AN INTERNAL EMPTINESS

The core problem is lack of self-esteem. The individual feels empty and worthless if not involved with a person or group. This internal sense of emptiness is based in the lack of positive experiences growing up in a non-nurturing, dysfunctional family. Developing personal worth and self-esteem is a prime task of childhood. The person who enters adulthood with low self-esteem or, in extreme cases, without a sense of self has a severe deficit. However, co-dependence is not the solution.

Self-esteem gradually develops from a range of competencies, learnings, experiences, and groups. Good friendships, and especially a stable and satisfying intimate relationship, facilitate self-esteem. A core tenet of self-esteem is it cannot be dependent on one source or external forces. You cannot use people, causes, groups, or objects (alcohol, food, sex, excitement, money) to fulfill you. The multiple sources, balanced approach to building and maintaining self-esteem lacks the pizazz of "pop psychology" gurus and recovery miracles. However, this approach is more successful and stable than simplistic, overpromising quick-fix cures. A healthy balance of competencies and relationships are the surest and most successful way to fill the internal emptiness.

INTERDEPENDENCE

Interdependence is the solution to the dilemma of alienation or co-dependence. Interdependence refers to the person's sense of personal worth so relationships develop from choice, not desperateness. Choose people, groups, and causes that enhance your life. The majority of people and groups are good, but there are 10–15% of people and groups who have negative motivations and cause major problems. One element of psychological well-being is the ability to discriminate who to become involved with and staying away from people and relationships which are "poison." You cannot choose your family, but you can choose friends, groups, and causes. Choose people you like and respect, and who care about you. The closer the relationship, the more important to choose well.

Clinicians' offices are full of people (usually women) who have solid friendships and are good judges of character—except when it comes to romantic/sexual relationships. As a culture, we have bought into the "romantic love" myth. People dream of being swept away by romantic, passionate feelings. Partner choice, including marriage, is controlled by emotion, idealizing the partner and relationship. What nonsense! Sexual attraction is important, but should not be the prime factor in choosing a partner. An intimate relationship, especially marriage, is primarily a respectful, trusting friendship with emotional and sexual attraction a necessary component. You are aware of the person's weaknesses as well as strengths. The commitment to share your lives is based on awareness and acceptance, not dreams and idealization.

The root of abusive, co-dependent relationships is the desperate need to find someone to love you. A charismatic person who promises an exciting, passionate relationship is very seductive. Romantic love mismatches are strongly reinforced by movies, novels, soap operas, and magazine stories. Initially they are exciting and intriguing, but ultimately result in painful break-ups and negation of self-esteem. "Hollywood romances" are usually fatally flawed. That's a harsh statement, but empirically true. The seductive, challenging element is compelling. For example, the co-dependent person puts her self-worth on the line to convert her lover. If he really loved her or she was good enough, he would stop drinking, stop being violent, and get a job instead of dealing drugs. In this case, the co-dependent person makes his problem hers. Changing his problem becomes the measure of her self-worth. What a self-defeating position!

A key concept involves personal boundaries. An individual with high self-esteem is aware of areas which are in her domain and control, and issues which are not hers. A friend gives feedback and is supportive, but realizes she cannot control the other person—it's that person's problem, not hers. The concept of boundaries, awareness of what is in your control and responsibility (and what is not) is crucial. Even the therapist must be aware of the concept of boundaries. He cares for clients, listens to their concerns and feelings, helps them explore alternatives and do effective problem solving, reduce negative motivations (fear, anger, depression), build comfort and skills—but ultimately it is the client's life and responsibility, not the clinician's. If someone as well-trained as a Ph.D. psychologist and paid for her services cannot assume ultimate responsibility for changing another person, why should you?

CIRCLES OF INTIMACY

One way to understand relationships is the concept of "circles of intimacy." You can categorize relationships based on five concentric circles starting with circle "E" on the outermost perimeter and narrowing to circle "A" at the core. "E" relationships refer to the entire range of people who cross your path—from passengers on a bus to a clerk in a store to people on the street. You don't know their names and relate in a rudimentary manner. You should be respectful and courteous, but there is no personal connection. In a typical day, you might encounter 500 people and in your lifetime hundreds of thousands of people in circle "E."

The first real personal contact comes with level "D" relationships—the acquaintance level. This refers to people whose names you know, have coffee with and talk about relevant topics (but not disclose personal or emotionally important issues). Extroverted people might have over 100 acquaintances at a given time and tens of thousands over a lifetime. People who are more discriminating in their relationship style might have twenty acquaintances at a time.

The first level involving a degree of emotional intimacy is "C" friendships. You share activities and feelings with friends and they are an important part of your life. Extroverted people might have twenty friends at a time and over 1,000 during their lifetime. Discriminating people might have less than five at a time and 100 during a lifetime. Friendships can last weeks or years, but when life circumstances change—you move, change jobs, get married—these friendships fade out. For a time you share a great deal with level "C" friends, but not your most intimate thoughts, feelings, or fears.

Level "B" refers to "special friendships," close relationships you care about and value. When life circumstances change, you pursue these friends and keep good contact. There is a high degree of self-disclosure and trust. Special friends share your most important experiences and feelings. Extroverted people might have ten special friends at a given time and 200 through a lifetime. More discriminating people might have two or less at one time and less than twenty over a lifetime. Special friendships are a major component in self-esteem.

Level "A" relationships are crucial. These include a spouse, best friend, mentor, confidante, a particularly close relationship with a parent or sibling. You are most self-disclosing, emotionally intimate, and vulnerable in a level "A" relationship. These are people who love and accept you for the person you are, with your strengths and weaknesses. Extroverted people might have seven level "A" relationships at a time and fifty over a lifetime. More discriminating people might have one or two at a time and five or ten over a lifetime. These relationships require the most trust and interdependence.

As the degree of emotional intimacy deepens, the importance and value of the relationship increases, but so too does the risk. When an acquaintance or friend becomes angry and breaks off the relationship it will hurt your feelings temporarily, but is unlikely to have a lasting effect. However, when a special friend or spouse angrily ends the relationship, there is a profound sense of loss, with a continuing impact on self-esteem. When couples divorce, the process of grieving the loss of the marriage, feelings of anger and resentment, and reorganizing your life and self-esteem can extend over a two-year period. Close relationships are of great importance—they reinforce self-esteem and add to the quality of life or subvert self-esteem and leave a wake of guilt, anger, blaming, and emptiness.

Ideally, one's parents and siblings would be in circle "B" or "A." Adults from dysfunctional families have to face the sad reality that family-of-origin relationships have been abusive, or at least disappointing. It is important for adults from dysfunctional families to choose respectful, trusting relationships.

People need quality relationships which give a sense of context, connection, and meaning to their lives. It is crucial to choose people and relationships which bring out healthy aspects of your personality while allowing you to retain individuality and responsibility. No relationship—to a person or group—should cause you to negate self-esteem. The key in recognizing if a relationship, cause, or group is co-dependent is if it causes you to act against your best interest. A relationship, cause, or group is healthy if it adds meaning and connection, allows you to be an independent person and is an important (but not controlling) element in self-esteem.

Exercise—Identifying Your Circles of Intimacy

Now that we have described the concept, let's make it personal. We suggest you do this exercise by yourself, and then share it with a close friend or spouse. Have four pieces of paper, one for each circle (there's no need to do this for circle "E"). For "D" circle you need not list all acquaintances, but think of the people you interact with from the neighborhood, job, extended family, sports or clubs, church or community organization. How many people are in your life? Are you comfortable with the way you relate? Do you enjoy groups and being gregarious, or are you more comfortable with fewer people and relating one-on-one? Are you an easy person to be with?

List "C" circle friends by name. Be aware of the number and quality of friendships. Which friendships are particularly valuable? Do some friends and activities subvert self-esteem? If so, these need to be changed or the friendship ended. Building and maintaining quality friendships enhances your life. Is there give-and-take or are you dependent?

Level "B," special friendships, are particularly important. How many close friends do you have, what percentage are same sex, how long has the friendship lasted, how often are you in contact, what do you do and talk about? Examine the patterns of close friendships. Some people find they have not developed a special friend in ten years, others discover all their close friends are of the opposite sex, others realize sports or partying are the only shared activities, some find they always do group or couple activities as opposed to one-on-one. Are you satisfied with the number and quality of special friendships?

"A" circle intimate relationships most affect self-esteem. How many people are in your "A" circle? What characteristics of the persons and relationships do you value? Do you respect and trust people in your "A" circle? Is the relationship reciprocal and interdependent? Can you self-disclose and discuss a range of feelings and experiences? Think of circle "A" relationships which have ended. Did they end in a good way or were you devastated?

Be aware of where you placed your parents, siblings, and other relatives. Are you comfortable with these relationships? Are there relatives you are alienated from with whom you wish to resume a relationship? Are there relatives you are too dependent on, and need to establish appropriate adult boundaries?

How do you assess the quantity and quality of your relationships? Are they give-and-take, interdependent relationships or is there too much dependence? This exercise is meant to increase awareness. If there are patterns of dependence or dissatisfaction, they need to be addressed. Identify the best relationships in each circle. Do they reflect genuine interdependence? Are you able to establish and maintain emotional connection and at the same time retain personal autonomy and boundaries?

INTERDEPENDENT RELATIONSHIPS

A level "D" relationship should not control self-esteem. You cannot give an acquaintance that much power. The more emotionally intimate the relationship, the greater the satisfaction, but more risk of dependence. The spouse who says "you need to love me" and "depend totally on me" is urging that not out of love, but from desperateness and fear of abandonment.

We advocate the "best friend" model of marriage, believing this meets intimacy and security needs in the healthiest manner. This assumes a marriage based on self-esteem, positive motivation, maintaining autonomy, having individual and couple friends, and a life apart from the spouse. A healthy marriage is "two strong trees joined to provide shade and nurturance" not "two weak saplings clinging together for survival (and interfering with the root system, therefore twisting branches and stunting growth)." A core concept is not to sacrifice yourself. An interdependent relationship allows the healthiest aspects of your personality to develop. Even during a crisis when you need a great deal of support, the spouse doesn't assume control. You are responsible for yourself.

If you ask a special friend to rescue you or your friend says you have to rescue him (whether from depression, alcoholism, abusive parenting, etc.), this relationship has crossed the line into co-dependence. A crucial element of interdependence is that both people maintain intact personal boundaries. You don't lose yourself and merge into another entity. Support is part of interdependence, rescuing and giving up part of co-dependence. Signals that the line of healthy relating has been crossed include doing things for friends that are not in your best interest, desperately clinging to the relationship, fear of being alone, well-being controlled by the relationship, feeling afraid of or for your partner, giving up friends and activities because the partner demands it, feeling blackmailed or intimidated, feeling empty and worthless without the person.

A PERSONAL NOTE

Theoretically, clinically, and personally we advocate a "best friend" model of marriage. We value our bond of respect, trust, and intimacy, and devote time and psychological energy to keeping our bond strong and vital. Marriage meets intimacy and security needs better than any other human relationship. Ideally, marriage involves two healthy people who value each other and their bond and have an interdependent relationship.

We consider each other spouse, lover, and best friend. We share experiences and feelings. However, the marriage does not account for more than a quarter of self-esteem. We do not merge, but maintain a sense of individuality and self-worth. There are times we lean on each other, but realize it's temporary and value being able to stand independently. We have no doubt that if one died, the other would survive and lead his/her life. However, we would sorely miss and mourn the spouse. One reason we value our bond is it's not burdened by desperateness or negative motivation. We know we can live separately, which enhances our togetherness because we choose to be together. Positive motivation is part of healthy interdependence, while negative motivation is an integral part of co-dependence.

We believe in the importance of both individual autonomy and a vital marital bond which promotes interdependence.

Jennifer and Alex. Jennifer and Alex were married seven years, had two children under five years of age, and were an example of a couple with a marginal marriage and a great deal of dependence. Co-dependence, low self-esteem, and marginal marriages tend to go together.

Jennifer was thirty-nine and married Alex partly out of fear she would never marry. She'd grown up in a dysfunctional family where Father was alcoholic, Mother depressed, and everyone pretended things were perfectly normal. Both of Jennifer's siblings were divorced. Alex was forty-two, had married at twenty-two, and his wife left and took their daughter. Two years later, his ex-wife remarried and the new husband adopted the daughter. Alex disliked being single, and was the "black sheep" in his family.

Fear motivation and feelings of personal weakness are core elements of co-dependence. Individual and couple growth is inhibited by fear it will lead to dissolution of the marriage and abandonment. Yet, a key to successful marriages is promoting individual and relationship growth. A marriage like Jennifer and Alex's will stay together, but be mired in conflict, resentment, and fear. The advice they received from the minister who had married them, and who for seven years heard their tales of conflict and dissatisfaction, was to seek marriage therapy. Couples caught in the cycle of low self-esteem and a co-dependent relationship find it almost impossible to change by themselves. The deciding factor was the minister saying it would not be healthy for their children to be raised in a tense, unhappy home. Jennifer did not want to pass the legacy of a dysfunctional family onto her children.

Jennifer assured Alex she did not have a hidden agenda to leave the marriage, but wanted to create a healthier, stronger marital bond. Jennifer was committed, but wanted a better quality life and family. She was empathic and understood Alex's fears of abandonment, but these fears kept the marriage stagnant.

Building a martial bond which promotes self-esteem and an interdependent relationship was a difficult, complex challenge. The hardest part was Jennifer confronting Alex in a constructive manner. Alex needed to deal with issues, but was strongly reactive to negative feedback and prone to withdraw. It was hard for him to remain in the present and deal with Jennifer's feelings and requests for change. Alex's automatic response was to react as he had with his family of origin and ex-wife. He expected to be rejected and abandoned, and so any negative feedback was personalized and responded to as if it was a catastrophe. Insight into this defensive pattern was important, but Alex needed more. His life, marriage, and family of creation couldn't be dominated by fears and past hurts. Jennifer couldn't be the perfect spouse who would never be disappointed or angry.

Alex needed to listen to Jennifer's feelings, perceptions, and requests and hear them for what they were, not through the shield of defensiveness. They had a signal where Jennifer would say "listen to what I'm saying now," to get Alex to focus. Jennifer valued the security and intimacy of marriage, but didn't want Alex to be her slave. She respected him when he maintained his sense of self.

Alex played on a community softball team for ten years. One of their best family times was bringing the children to the games and afterwards having a cookout with other families. Jennifer respected Alex's professional competence and skill at household tasks—neighbors often asked his advice on electrical and plumbing problems. The thing Jennifer respected least was his defensiveness and desperate clinging.

Jennifer had to confront a different set of issues. Her tendency was to go to extremes. Most of the time she was overly giving, concerned, and took responsibility for solving Alex's problems, her children's problems, and those of friends and family. However, when she felt burned out she went to the opposite extreme of feeling fed up and resentful. This was manifested by impulsively leaving the house and not returning until the early morning. This frightened Alex and the children. Jennifer vacillated between feeling justified and guilty about her emotional acting out. Jennifer's goal was to be aware of and express feelings rather than impulsively act on them.

A key strategy was that at least once a month Jennifer planned a day to herself or with friends. Anticipating this time gave her a life outside the spouse, parent, supportive caretaker role. In the past, she'd always put the needs of others over hers. Now Jennifer tries to follow the therapeutic guideline of taking care of her needs and then attending to the marriage and parenting. Jennifer was afraid of shortchanging the children, but found when her life is on track and the marriage is doing well, the children benefit from being parented by two involved, loving people.

A residual issue is that Jennifer wishes life could be easier. She realizes, however, the importance of realistic expectations and celebrating the positive while being able to talk about and deal with problems. Alex maintains their life is more interesting and challenging (even if hectic and stressful) than their families of origin and he wouldn't trade it. Co-dependent marriages are stable and predictable, but stifling to individual and couple growth. The interdependent marriage Jennifer and Alex established was complicated, but satisfying. It allowed for individual strengths, growth, and vulnerabilities while maintaining the integrity of their marital bond.

THE NECESSITY TO CONFRONT
CO-DEPENDENT RELATIONSHIPS

It's hard to change a co-dependent relationship—is it worth the time and effort? The answer is not an unequivocal yes. Many people place a high value on stability and predictability. The fear, which is not unwarranted, is that the relationship can be destroyed by examination and confrontation. However, like

Jennifer and Alex, a couple can affirm their commitment while breaking the suffocating cycle of dependence and fear of abandonment. Our culture puts too much emphasis on being in a relationship (especially for women); being single carries an inordinate fear and stigma. People cling to destructive or marginal relationships to avoid being on their own. The person must realize his or her own worth whether single or married, in a relationship or not.

Children from dysfunctional families are more likely to thrive if at least one parent has positive self-esteem. Co-dependent relationships might be secure and predictable, but they drain self-esteem. It is worthwhile for the person, marriage, and family to address the co-dependence issue in a productive manner.

An oft-heard objection is that the person becomes so involved in the co-dependence problem and 12-step groups that a worse problem is created. Although this certainly happens, it is the exception. The common pattern is to become aware of the problem, realize it's multicausal—having elements of both the past and present—and addressing it so self-esteem improves. The result is healthier, interdependent relationships, not the elimination of relationships. Going from one extreme to the other is not the path to psychological well-being. The key is to develop awareness and self-respect. Balance individual needs with those of others. Learn to choose well and act in your best interests.

CLOSING THOUGHTS

Co-dependence is a new concept that has had an overwhelming response, especially in the media and 12-step programs. There are a multitude of groups and books focused on co-dependence. We believe there is a continuum with the alienated, isolated person on one extreme and the desperate, needy co-dependent person on the other. Individual differences and life circumstances are variable; there is no ideal place on the independence/dependence continuum which would be healthy for everyone. The goal is to establish personal worth and self-esteem and choose relationships which are healthy and interdependent.

Labeling people and problems co-dependent is an overgeneralization which hinders understanding and change. The label co-dependent has lost its meaning. It's used to stigmatize and "blame the victim." The way to empower a person is to make her aware of self-worth, the need to take responsibility, and to choose relationships which bring out the best in her and enhance her life.

11
TWELVE-STEP GROUPS

Twelve-Step programs began with Alcoholics Anonymous and now encompass more than thirty different types of groups. It is the largest, fastest growing phenomenon in the mental health field and shows no sign of slowing down. The 12 steps are viewed as a panacea for almost any kind of problem. There is no doubt that hundreds of thousands of people have received great benefit from self-help groups using the 12-step program as well as other models.

There are strengths in self-help groups which surpass the benefits available through professional psychotherapy. Being in a group with people experiencing the same problem reduces stigma. The group provides an accepting milieu that reduces the shame and secrecy which are so destructive to self-esteem. It provides a steady, consistent source of support. Group members who succeed in changing their lives provide a positive model and source of hope. A sponsor providing guidance and support can be of particular benefit. In the group, the person learns new attitudes, skills, and ways to express emotions healthily.

The answer to the question of whether 12-step groups can help is yes. The answer to the question of whether they are being oversold as helpful to everyone and every problem is, unfortunately, also yes. Twelve-step programs are being promoted as the *only* effective treatment for addictions, childhood trauma, and compulsive behavior. This is both scientifically inaccurate and clinically wrong. People who are not comfortable or successful with the 12-step approach are labeled failures and told they have to work the program or their lives will remain out of control. A prime guide in health and mental health is "First do no harm." The overpromise and rigidity of some 12-step adherents are iatrogenic. This means in trying to cure a problem you inadvertently create a different and more severe problem. People who do not benefit from 12-step programs feel like failures and become hopeless. The truth is that 12-step programs do not work for all people or problems.

The 12-step group with the strongest tradition and most comprehensive program is AA—Alcoholics Anonymous. Alcohol use is easily defined and the goal of abstinence easily evaluated. The traditional approach maintains that you are always a "recovering alcoholic," you can never drink, and must remain actively involved in 12-step groups for the rest of your life. Although there is a dearth of scientific follow-up data, even AA's strongest advocates acknowledge success rates (using total abstinence and continued 12-step involvement as the criterion) are less than thirty percent. Most researchers believe the rate is less than fifteen percent. Does that mean AA has been of no value to 85% of the people who have turned to it for help? Absolutely not. What it does mean is that the ideal of how the program is supposed to work is dramatically different from the reality of how it actually works for most people.

What does this mean for groups like Adult Children of Alcoholics and Co-Dependents Anonymous? In these groups the definition of the problem is much more ambiguous and criterion of success (abstinence) is almost impossible to define. Most troubling is the admonition to continue to work the program, attend groups, and interpret a range of difficulties and issues through the 12-step model. This can foster an unhealthy dependence and self-definition as a victim.

THE RIGHT QUESTION ABOUT
12-STEP PROGRAMS

In the field of Recovery and Adult Children, it is easy, but wrong, to take simplistic stances. Human behavior is complex, multicausal, and multidimensional. There is nothing that can be said in a self-help group, in therapy, or in a book that is correct for every person, relationship, or situation. Individuals, couples, and families have unique strengths and problems. The right question is what kind of intervention, with what kind of person or relationship, at what time, in what circumstances, and for how long, is most helpful? This is not an easy yes-no question. There are tremendous differences in the quality of 12-step groups, the match between the individual's needs and the way the group functions, and availability of professional and other self-help resources.

Self-help groups are valuable for many, if not most, people. Their greatest contribution is as a safe, accepting place to share experiences which had been secret, thus reducing stigma and shame. The group allows the person to see how others have dealt with issues and experience being supported and supporting others. Twelve-step programs are the most common and best organized self-help groups, but not the only type. Examples of other groups are Weight-Watchers, Parents of Handicapped Children, Compassionate Friends (for parents whose children have died), and support groups for various illnesses such as cancer, AIDS, or diabetes.

Twelve-step programs stress ongoing, if not lifetime, commitment. Most people need at least four months in a self-help group to understand the message and incorporate it into their lives. Many find remaining in the group for more than six months is not beneficial. They received the information and support and feel ready to move on to the next chapter of their lives. This guideline is most relevant for Adult Children groups. Groups such as AA, Gamblers Anonymous, or Batters Anonymous usually require longer-term involvement. A non-12-step self-help group for alcoholics, Rational Recovery, advises people to move on from the group after a year so they don't become dependent.

There are people who remain in 12-step groups for five, ten, twenty-five years and longer. Twelve-step groups have become an integral part of their lives. Some view it as a substitute family. They are involved in sponsoring new members and assume a leadership position. Others find the continued support and structure necessary to keep their lives on track.

An objection many people, including therapists, have to 12-step programs is the emphasis on continuing participation and defining yourself by the problem. When people feel ready to leave, they experience disapproval and sometimes coercion to remain. It is true that stopping involvement in a recovery program can be a sign of denial or poor judgment, but for many it is a healthy realization that they have dealt with the problem and are ready for new involvements and commitments. The truth of the human condition is that there are seldom total cures. As the person's life and circumstances change, new issues and challenges arise.

ARE THERE PEOPLE WHO DO NOT BENEFIT FROM 12-STEP PROGRAMS?

As noted earlier, in medicine a prime rule is "First do no harm." The concept of iatrogenic damage is receiving increasing attention in health and mental health. That is, problems (often more serious) are unintentionally caused by trying to cure a different problem. An example is the experience of a person who enters an Adult Child group to deal with growing up in an abusive family. As she becomes aware of memories, pain, and trauma, she feels overwhelmed by pathology. She feels like a victim and acts out the victim role in her life and relationships. She becomes depressed or alcoholic, her marriage breaks up, she is a neglectful or abusive parent, loses her job, is hospitalized—her life becomes increasingly out of control. Was this caused by childhood abuse or the inability to deal with adult issues? Did she focus so much time and psychological energy on the pain and trauma of the past that she felt overwhelmed and her life went out of control?

A second, less common, example is an obsessive-compulsive personality entering a 12-step program. He strives to be perfect, which means total abstinence in thought, fantasy, word, and deed. If he feels he's made any mistakes, he develops elaborate rituals to undo the wrong. He goes to two or three meetings a day, has multiple sponsors, and makes innumerable phone calls. Rather than the 12-step program leading to recovery, it has become part of an elaborate self-defeating, compulsive ritual.

These examples demonstrate that 12-step programs and self-help groups are not for everyone. They can be iatrogenic. Especially problematic are people who misuse 12-step programs when they would benefit from a different intervention such as professional psychotherapy (individual, couple, group, family) or a psycho-educational, time-limited program to develop skills (assertiveness, parenting, couple communications, or anger management).

There are at least three categories of people who should not enter 12-step groups (especially those dealing with childhood victimization). These are people with obsessive-compulsive personality traits, highly suggestible people who are prone to over-generalize, and rigid, rule-directed individuals. Twelve-step groups for those people are often iatrogenic. Of course, there are exceptions.

Human behavior is complex, multicausal, and individualistic. No one approach has a corner on rightness or helpfulness. In deciding what is helpful and what to avoid, consider the following guidelines.

GUIDELINES FOR CHOOSING
A 12-STEP PROGRAM

Twelve-step programs are most effective in addressing specific addictive or compulsive behaviors. That's what they were designed for and what they do best. Groups with a history of success and stability, a tradition of caring, involved sponsors, and regular, well-structured meetings are most helpful. Examples include Alcoholics Anonymous and Debtors Anonymous. On the other end of the continuum are newly formed, nebulous groups where it is hard to define both the problem and the criterion for abstinence—these include Emotions Anonymous and Sex Addicts Anonymous. Although specific groups might be well-structured with a good cadre of sponsors and clear rules, many are confused and disorganized, with arbitrary and unrealistic standards of abstinence. With alcohol it's clear what the bottom line is—you drink or you don't. What is the bottom line for emotions, co-dependence, or sex?

A second type of 12-step program is helping those whose lives have been affected indirectly by the addiction. The oldest and best example is Al-Anon. This was based on the concept of alcoholism as a family disease, affecting not only the alcoholic, but other family members. Al-Anon involves spouses and sometimes parents and siblings. Rather than "enabling" the alcoholic by covering up and compensating, the spouse is encouraged to "disengage." The alcoholic needs to confront his addiction and commit to abstinence. The spouse and other relatives disengage and not let their lives be controlled by alcoholism. Ala-Teen was established for teenagers who have an alcoholic or recovering alcoholic parent to receive support and deal with their lives, including not abusing alcohol or drugs.

Adult Children of Alcoholics is by far the largest of the 12-step groups for those affected by a parent's problems. The child grew up in an alcoholic family where reality was denied and feelings were "stuffed." The goal is to use the 12-step program to promote the adult child's recovery from growing up in a dysfunctional family. This has spawned a number of 12-step programs including Adult Children of Dysfunctional Families, Co-Dependents Anonymous, Adult Children of Neglect and Abuse, Adult Children of Divorce, Grandchildren of Alcoholics. The problem with some of these groups is the lack of structure and clear goals, obsessive focus on the past, and sense of victimization, blaming, and anger (very different from the concept of disengagement). Major drawbacks are the open-ended nature of these groups and the theme of relating all adult problems to childhood trauma.

As children grow up they want freedom and responsibility.

As adults, does it make sense to become stuck in childhood conflicts and resentments? Is remaining in an Adult Child group for two years or longer helping the person be a survivor?

There are special issues and problems caused by growing up in an alcoholic, abusive, or dysfunctional family. Self-help groups allow the person to confront shame and guilt, increase awareness of issues and psychological traps, and motivate people to establish a family of creation which is loving and stable. Some groups facilitate this process, but others are iatrogenic. The goal of Al-Anon is to help family members disengage from the alcohol (dysfunctional behavior) and lead satisfying lives. Some Adult Child groups, however, reinforce childhood victimization, resulting in past trauma and abuse controlling adult life.

The question to ask about the 12-step group you're considering entering (or are reevaluating) is whether it promotes self-esteem and helps you be a survivor. Be open to input from the group and sponsor, but remember that ultimately it is your decision. Act in your best interests. What do you need to learn about the past? What do you have to do to put your life on a functional, satisfying path? What resources help keep your life on track?

A major function of self-help groups is to confront denial and deal with guilt, secrecy, and shame. People are urged to enter a 12-step program which emphasizes abstinence from abusive, addictive behaviors and living a responsible, spiritual life. Choose a group and sponsor that matches your personality and goals. Be sure the group has a positive structure and is neither coercive nor punishing. You need confrontation and support, not punishment or someone controlling you. Survivors are responsible for themselves, not controlled by past trauma or dictates of the group.

Does the group recognize individual differences or do they advocate one unbending program? Do people move through the program, staying as long as needed or do they become dependent? In the first weeks of a 12-step group there is information, structure, and support. As the program continues, is there room for individual issues and needs or does the rigorous structure continue? When people leave the group, is it accepted or treated with hostility and accusations? Do they demand you give up your individuality to meet group norms?

Not all groups are the same. There are groups where it appears the "blind lead the blind." Other groups are dominated by power struggles. Some groups are controlled by the pain or pathology of one or two members. Sometimes political fights and personality clashes subvert the work of self-help groups.

There is not an ideal group which fits the needs of all people. Here are some key points to keep in mind: 1) choose a group that has a tradition of stability and success, 2) be sure the group is focused and small enough, 3) there is a solid cadre of sponsors, 4) choose a sponsor who respects your needs, 5) be sure the group will allow you to cut back or leave without coercion to stay.

PROFESSIONAL PSYCHOTHERAPY AND 12-STEP GROUPS—ANTAGONISTS OR COMPLEMENTARY?

There is a legacy of antagonism between the field of psychotherapy and self-help groups. The joke among professionals was that AA groups "needed someone to fall off the wagon so they could be saviors." AA was viewed as an alternate dependency, better than drinking, but a sign of weakness. Many recovering alcoholics who had been in psychotherapy with unsuccessful results had an anti-professional bias, the joke being "therapists were too stupid to see the real problem was alcoholism." The patients believed the only person who could understand and treat an alcoholic was a recovering alcoholic. Professionals were viewed as naive and overpaid.

The war between professionals and 12-step advocates is silly and unnecessary. Both can contribute to change. The need to confront addictive or destructive behavior is universally accepted. Since it is easier to stop (whether drinking, gambling, drug use, or smoking) than moderate the behavior, abstinence is the preferred goal. Twelve-step advocates believe it has to be the goal for all addictive and compulsive behaviors, while professional opinion is split. There are some people and some behaviors where moderation and control have been reestablished, although the person has to be motivated and rigorous in maintaining it. There are people who attend AA, abstain from drinking for months or years, and return to moderate drinking—some with minimal difficulty, while others regress to out-of-control drinking. Other compulsive behaviors (eating, sex, emotional expression) require confronting destructive patterns, but replacing them with healthier behaviors.

For addictive behavior we recommend both professional therapy and a 12-step program. The initial intervention is to confront denial and make a commitment to change; this is the forte of self-help groups. For adults dealing with childhood abuse our recommendation is professional therapy with 12-step or other self-help programs as an adjunct. We realize this is a conservative and unpopular approach. It is not a universal recommendation. The desires, resources, and circumstances of the individual or family are crucial in deciding the best way to promote change.

Psychotherapy is particularly valuable for adults dealing with an abusive childhood. Therapy helps the client utilize resources in the most productive manner and keeps the focus on being a survivor rather than caught in the victimization cycle. The therapist can help her decide how to best utilize books, groups, and the sponsor relationship. She is empowered to ignore aspects of the program that are not relevant or could be iatrogenic.

Erica and Mark. Erica is twenty-eight years old, married for three years to twenty-seven-year-old Mark, and they have a one-year-old son. They entered therapy at the advice of Erica's sponsor after Mark threatened to end the marriage. Erica and Mark had a romantic, passionate, and intense courtship. Although they'd been a couple sixteen months before marrying, they had not discussed family of origin or difficult life issues. They focused on love and longing. They believed "love would conquer all"—a self-defeating, yet seductive, cultural myth. Whenever there was a problem, it was resolved through an intense sexual encounter.

The relationship began changing shortly after Erica became pregnant. Their son was planned and wanted, but Mark found the idea of being responsible for another human being overwhelming. He viewed his own parents as too child-focused and was afraid individual and couple plans would be subverted by parenthood.

With Erica's pregnancy, Mark felt his fears had been confirmed. He questioned Erica's commitment and ability to be a good mother. Erica joined an Adult Children of Dysfunctional Families group six months into the pregnancy and, for reasons entirely different from Mark's, worried about parenting. Erica was afraid she would be like her mother—often angry and abusive and at other times neglectful and withdrawn. Between Mark's negative reactions and her feelings of victimization and helplessness, Erica felt life was becoming unmanageable.

When Erica and Mark appeared for their first therapy session, the tension was palpable. They were a devitalized, angry, and blaming couple. Mark was on the attack, saying if he'd known what Erica was really like he'd never have married her. Erica was suffering from low self-esteem, depressed by insights into her dysfunctional family, a marriage that was disintegrating, overwhelmed by forthcoming motherhood, and difficulties balancing work and parenting. The only person who Erica felt understood her was her sponsor in the self-help group, and that person was becoming overwhelmed in the role of Erica's substitute mother. Mark was particularly bitter that he and Erica had only made love twice in the past three months. Although the 12-step group increased Erica's awareness, it was not improving her functioning and was adding to marital stress. Mark was a blamer. A favorite target was Erica's 12-step group, saying she preferred it to marriage and family.

It's hard to write about psychotherapy because therapy is such a complex, subtle, and individualistic process. Therapy is valuable in a way psychology self-help books can't be.

There were three clients—Mark, Erica, and their marital

bond. Ideally, psychotherapy improves each person's self-esteem and marital satisfaction. The therapist realized he had two unhappy people locked in a power struggle that would destroy their marriage, and made his usual suggestion—Mark and Erica commit to a six-month "good faith" effort to revitalize the marital bond and commit to making significant personal changes. Mark was surprised to hear he would need to change and was taken aback by the therapist's observation that his anger and judgmentalness were subverting the marital bond.

After the couple meeting, an individual session with each was scheduled. In discussing Mark's background, it became clear he didn't trust women nor did he have an appropriate model for the balance between self-esteem, marriage, and family. Mark's behavior was governed by fear—of being dominated, abandoned, or played a fool by Erica. He expressed these fears through put-downs and threats. Mark had idealized Erica and put her on a pedestal during their premarital year. Since the marriage he was bitterly disappointed and angry. He viewed the 12-step program as making excuses for Erica. Mark blamed Erica for all the problems. The therapist's assessment was that Mark had an intimacy disorder, an inability to form and maintain an intimate relationship. Mark was at first defensive, but in thinking about it accepted the diagnosis. Erica had to address her problems, but if Mark were not willing to address his intimacy issues, it would destroy this marriage and he would repeat this self-defeating pattern in subsequent relationships.

Erica was willing to address problems, but every new insight and issue became a severe problem. When Erica heard of group members' family or parenting problems, she reacted as if they were hers. The therapist had a phone consultation with Erica's sponsor, who was quite concerned about Erica's life. The sponsor agreed Erica should cut back her 12-step commitment to one meeting a week and encouraged Erica (as did the therapist) to join a fifteen-session support group for mothers of children under two after the baby was born. Erica needed to rebuild self-esteem, develop a relationship with Mark where he was her supporter, not worst critic, and improve parenting skills. She needed to examine her family of origin and identify both vulnerabilities and strengths. Her assessments so far had been global and subjective, and didn't guide her in making decisions or changes. She was too harsh in her judgments and too frightened of the mother role. After the baby was born, the mothers' support group was powerfully validating—Erica learned her new son's behavior was in the normal range and that she was responding appropriately.

The therapist emphasized the necessity of rebuilding respect, trust, and intimacy between Erica and Mark. This was a slower, more complex process than jumping into bed and having passionate sex. He encouraged them to resume their affectionate and sexual relationship, which helped reenergize the marital bond. However, sex cannot substitute for respect and trust. Even the most sexually satisfied couple have to deal with difficult issues.

Erica again felt connected to Mark, but didn't want to return to the pedestal. She was a worthwhile human being, with strengths and vulnerabilities. Erica desired a secure marital bond and a loving, cohesive three-person family. At a session of the support group, there was to be a speaker on dysfunctional families who Erica thought would be particularly insightful, and invited Mark to accompany her to the presentation. Mark realized the group (or at least that speaker and Erica's sponsor) were not anti-marriage. Erica appreciated Mark's new attitude, but realized she'd misused the group to reinforce feelings of being a vulnerable victim, needing to be rescued. She'd engaged in a great deal of self-pity and blaming, and the group had colluded with this self-defeating approach.

Erica had been sexually abused and emotionally neglected as a child. Her approach to life, relationships, and sexuality had been to deny vulnerabilities and hard issues. The combination of individual and couple therapy, along with the self-help group and support of her sponsor, allowed Erica to address these issues. She was committed to building self-esteem, a viable marriage, and nurturing family of creation.

Without Mark's involvement their marriage would have become a divorce statistic. Not all marriages can or should be saved; there are fatally flawed marriages which subvert self-esteem. Erica and Mark had a viable marital bond, although it had been greatly stressed. Mark's willingness to address fears, anger, and intimacy problems were necessary to turn the marriage around. As Mark became less judgmental and angry, he was open to suggestions from the therapist, group and, most importantly, Erica.

The change process is not simple or straightforward. Therapy, 12-step programs, and other self-help groups can be complementary, but there needs to be understanding and cooperation. It is easy for these programs to work at cross-purposes. A trap people fall into (Erica was an example) is to identify so many problems and get so much conflicting advice from so many people that they feel overwhelmed. Awareness and problem solving are functional; feeling victimized and out of control results in demoralization and giving up. Erica and Mark realized maintaining a vital, satisfying marital bond takes continued psychological energy and attention. Self-esteem and marriage cannot rest on their laurels.

INTEGRATION OF PSYCHOTHERAPY
AND SELF-HELP GROUPS

A combination of psychotherapy and self-help groups is the treatment of choice for many people. Psychotherapy deals with complex, individual issues better than self-help groups. But both are more helpful than the best self-help book. The strength of self-help groups is reducing stigma, providing social support, an ongoing, structured program, and practical help and advice. One of the most valuable aspects is the sponsor who serves as a model and mentor.

Some therapists are so supportive of 12-step programs their input is redundant. Others are so skeptical, the client is caught in a power struggle between therapy and the group. Choose a therapist who is aware of strengths and weaknesses of self-help programs. The therapist can function as a consultant on how you can benefit from the group, as well as point out traps where the group ideology or advice is not relevant or helpful.

It is crucial to choose a therapist and self-help group that promote being a survivor and encourage you to lead a healthy, satisfying life in the present rather than using past trauma as an excuse. Some therapists and self-help programs inadvertently encourage the person to wallow in victimization and self-pity. This is not in your best interest. The goals of therapy and self-help groups are congruent and complementary—to address problems and promote psychological well-being.

Donna. Donna is a twenty-eight-year-old single woman, a veteran of social activist programs, who had no experience with therapy or self-help groups, and was suspicious of both. She had marched against rape, petitioned for child abuse laws, and wrote letters to the newspaper protesting violence against women. Donna had sex with both men and women, viewed herself as sexually aware and liberated, and labeled herself a political lesbian.

Her older brother, recently divorced, came for a visit. He was seeing a therapist for depression and was in a 12-step group, Debtors Anonymous. Donna was concerned for him, but he said the worst was over and he'd taken back control of his life. He'd felt devastated when his wife left with the complaints he was always worried and depressed and got his kicks from eating and spending. Donna believed women should leave dysfunctional marriages, but never realized until now how hard this was on the man. She was angry at the ex-wife for abandoning her brother rather than confronting and helping with the change process. He'd found psychotherapy of great value in changing his depressive attitudes and behavior. Debtors Anonymous helped him come to grips with the stigma of bankruptcy and learn to manage credit, bills, and money.

In a gentle, yet confrontative, manner he asked Donna about her life. He explained to her that he'd handled negative feelings by becoming depressed and engaging in self-defeating behavior. He asked her whether her system was to externalize and not think enough about herself and the direction of her life. Donna didn't want her political beliefs co-opted by "psychobabble,'' but realized she avoided sad feelings and had stronger feelings about political causes than personal issues.

Donna began to attend a self-help group for women with sexual concerns. The level of personal sharing, pain, and support was impressive. This approach was more impactful than the 12-step sexual abuse groups or social action groups against rape she'd heard about. A group session focused on ambivalence caused Donna to feel confused and anxious. She decided to see a credentialed, well-regarded feminist psychologist for individual therapy.

The therapeutic process of empathic listening, confrontation with difficult issues, and exploring ambivalence was difficult, yet worthwhile. Donna was surprised to discover family-of-origin and sexual issues were crucial. Her brother's hypothesis about externalizing was on target. Donna's tendency was to act, not explore perceptions or feelings. The therapist did not argue political beliefs, but encouraged her to understand and confront personal issues. The self-help group challenged her lesbianism, and the therapist agreed that sexual intimacy and orientation was personal, not political. Sexual orientation is a strong emotional and sexual attraction to either the same sex (homosexuality) or the opposite sex (heterosexuality). Donna realized her attraction was to men, but feared the difficulty in creating a satisfying intimate relationship with a man. The group shared her hopes and fears of making a relationship work in our culture, which values romantic love and sexual expression more than emotional and sexual intimacy. Donna found psychotherapy and the self-help group complemented her social and political beliefs, while causing her to confront and explore personal "blind spots."

CLOSING THOUGHTS

Neither psychotherapy nor self-help groups are panaceas. Twelve-step groups have gained phenomenal popularity in the past few years, not all of it deserved. When 12-step programs (or psychotherapy) reinforce the sense of victimization, they are iatrogenic. Ideally, psychotherapy and self-help groups would be complementary. They facilitate the confrontation with the secrecy and shame of an abusive childhood and enable the person to see herself as a survivor, live a life of self-esteem, and establish a healthy and satisfying family of creation rather than a dysfunctional life and family that continue the victimization cycle. People can use resources—professional and self-help, friends, relatives, spouse—to build responsible, satisfying lives. The confrontation and change process is difficult, but worthwhile. Be aware of negative sources that keep you stuck in the victim role (these include unethical or incompetent professionals, books that give bad advice and overpromise, groups that allow members to wallow in anger or self-pity, and programs that go nowhere or are inappropriate for your problem). Choose a therapist and/or a self-help group which promotes healing and psychological well-being.

12
POP PSYCHOLOGY GURUS VS. PSYCHOTHERAPY

In an undergraduate course, "Psychology of Well-Being," a student asked what "pop psychology" meant. The student's father said she was "buying into all that pop psychology junk." What is scientifically valid and what is pop psychology?

Pop psychology means popular psychology—ideally, the task of taking reliable, valid academic and clinical psychology findings and translating them so they can be understood and utilized by the public. A worthwhile goal. A generation ago the president of the American Psychological Association urged academics and professionals to "give psychology away." This noble goal has been lost in a blizzard of books, magazine articles, testimonials, and talk show "psychobabble."

Pop psychology, adult child, and recovery books and gurus have swept book stores and talk shows. Perhaps as many as fifty percent of these books are silly and irrelevant—not helpful, but at least not causing harm. However, twenty to twenty-five percent are harmful—setting self-defeating, unrealistic expectations and giving bad information and advice. The modus operandi of pop psychology gurus is simplistic advice, a charismatic writer and speaker, presenting inspiring case studies with miracle cures. They are exciting to listen to and read, but set a person up to feel dysfunctional and fail at the change process.

Pop psychology books on addictions, adult children, recovery, and co-dependence are prime examples of harmful materials. They promise much more than they deliver. Quizzes and tests to determine whether you have a problem or fall into a dysfunctional category are usually invalid, using unreliable scientific criteria. Not surprisingly, most readers fall into one or more dysfunctional categories. The joke is that 97% of people test as co-dependent, and the rest are in denial. Being a victim is encouraged. You feel left out if you can't identify personal or family pathology. It is healthy to confront problems and vulnerabilities, and it's helpful to realize you are not alone. However, these books encourage you to define yourself by the abuse and see all adult problems as rooted in childhood trauma. Scientifically and clinically that's nonsense.

The major damage done by pop psychology books and recovery gurus is promising a simple, total cure. Once you break silence/denial, join a 12-step group, and work the program, you will reach peace and serenity and live happily ever after. If you don't, it means you're in denial, haven't attended enough meetings, or worked hard enough at your program. For most people in most circumstances, this is crazy-making advice.

Rehashing the same strategies that didn't work the first or second time makes the person feel deficient and hopeless. A characteristic of psychological well-being is flexible, competent problem solving. The majority of self-help books are simplistic and rigid. Gurus promise the world if you only listen to their three (or twelve) rules for living. Human beings and life circumstances are too complex and varied for rigid rules. Awareness and psychological guidelines are of great value, but need to be individually tailored and applied.

THE SEDUCTIVENESS OF GURUS

Pop psychology gurus are not unlike television evangelists—sincere but misguided or out for self-aggrandizement with a corrupt hidden agenda. Self-help, recovery, and adult child gurus seduce their audiences with simple, black-and-white rules and sensationalistic stories of horrible childhoods and families, followed by golden stories of recovery, peace, and joy. Psychotherapists are optimistic about people's ability to deal with abuse and trauma, but realize it's a complex, gradual process with few miracle cures. Therapists have training in the scientific method and make a point of examining outcome data. Gurus make a point to avoid science and outcome data. Their approach is closer to the TV pitch—promising what can be packaged into a thirty-second commercial. Gurus speak in media "sound bites," seductive and entertaining. When people are confused or in pain, the easy answer that promises everything will be okay is very appealing.

Gurus play two important roles. Through speeches, writing, and talk show appearances they legitimize a problem and give it a high profile. Second, they motivate people and promote hope for change. They make people feel good—the person is worthwhile and "somebody." Maintaining motivation is key in changing life patterns. A harmful legacy of growing up in a dysfunctional family is that it robs the person of hope that things can be better. If the parent becomes worse—is jailed, hospitalized, or attempts suicide—the child becomes pessimistic and hopeless. Adults who grew up in dysfunctional families are reactive to negative feedback and give up too easily. Gurus confront, entreat, and energize the person who has given up.

Unfortunately, the guru's message feeds the disappointment/failure cycle. The guru sets expectations too high (total cure and perfect serenity) and makes the healing process sound too easy (confront the denial, enter a 12-step program and everything will be fine). People are frustrated and disillusioned to find not only is the change process difficult, but sometimes things get worse before they get better. Addiction problems, for example, are seldom cured on the first go-around. Relapse occurs in over 80% of cases. Maintaining motivation, having realistic goals, and being consistent are crucial. This is not the charismatic message of gurus.

THE VALUE OF PSYCHOTHERAPY

Mental health can be a complex, confusing field. There are a number of practitioners—clinical and counseling psychologists, clinical social workers, marriage and family therapists, psychiatrists, pastoral counselors, alcoholism and drug counselors. There are a range of services—individual, couple, family, and group therapy—and a number of theoretical orientations—cognitive, behavioral, family systems, psychodynamic, existential—to name just a few. Most important, however, is that training, competence, and experience varies widely. Appendix I of this book presents guidelines for choosing a therapist who is right for you.

When you choose a therapist, he or she should have training and competence in your area of concern; you should feel rapport and trust; and the assessment and proposed treatment plan should make sense.

Adults dealing with abuse and dysfunctional families need a therapist who is able to address both problems of the past and present-day issues. Be wary of the therapist who only wants to deal with family dynamics or "inner child" issues (unless that's your goal). Question the therapist who doesn't want to hear the pain and hurt of the past. A good therapist is respectful and caring of your needs, and uses clinical judgment in helping you change. A skilled clinician interweaves past and present issues in a manner which increases awareness and ability to deal with life and relationships. The therapist respects you and is aware of your complexity and individuality. In psychotherapy, the needs of the person transcend theory or ideology.

A common question is whether to consult someone who advertises expertise in Adult Child issues. There are excellent therapists who conduct focused, time-limited groups for Adult Children of Alcoholics or Adults Who Experienced Incest. There is a real advantage in group psychotherapy of having a common focus. However, be sure to carefully inquire about the clinician's credentials, training, and goals. Many poorly trained counselors and therapists with a strong ideological (as opposed to clinical) bent have jumped on the Adult Child bandwagon. Be sure the clinician is aware of your feelings and goals and her approach is compatible.

COUPLES THERAPY

Another common question is individual vs. couples therapy. Psychotherapy, especially psychodynamic therapy, traditionally emphasizes individual treatment. It is crucial to increase understanding and develop self-esteem. However, for married individuals, issues and conflicts are often best approached as a couple problem. Couples therapy can be a powerful intervention which improves self-esteem, the marital bond, parenting, and family relationships. The spouse can be helpful in developing a loving, responsible approach to life and family of creation. The spouse's perspective and emotional support can facilitate a healthier relationship with family of origin and heal wounds of the past.

A common intervention is to confront the competitive, put-down pattern couples fall into when discussing in-laws. Arguing which family is more dysfunctional and, in the midst of a fight, calling the spouse names is destructive. Choosing a therapy approach requires assessment, reflection, and awareness. There are no easy formulas in psychotherapy. It requires consideration of individual, couple, and family needs as well as clinical judgment to find the right therapeutic match.

Spouse abuse is a problem which, in most cases, is best dealt with as a couple, with a clinician whose expertise is family violence. The optimal intervention is a semi-structured group program focused on breaking the cycle of spousal violence. However, if one spouse subverts the process by threats and intimidation this can turn couples therapy into a sham.

There are conflicting ideologies about spouse abuse—from the idea that the sanctity of the marital bond must be preserved no matter what to one incident is enough for divorce. Not all couples experiencing spouse abuse are the same. No matter what gurus and self-help books say, the clinician has to attend to the needs of that couple. Effective psychotherapy requires assessment, clinical judgment, and individualized intervention. Psychotherapy focuses on clinical, not ideological issues, and tries to meet the needs and goals of the individual, couple, and family.

FAMILY THERAPY

Family therapy has become increasingly popular, especially with parent-child problems. Family therapists emphasize the importance of the family of origin and probe the roots of abuse and dysfunctional family systems. The therapist often suggests sessions with adults and their parents. The couple needs to be clear about goals and trust the therapist's skill and judgment. Family therapy is particularly powerful in confronting secrets, poor communication, and dysfunctional family patterns. When a family systems intervention works it can be powerful and healing. Therapy allows each member to assume responsibility for his/her behavior and establish healthier modes of communication and family interaction.

Family therapy is the treatment of choice where there has been incestuous activity. Incest is the "shameful family secret"—secrecy allows abusive sexual activity to continue. Lines of communication about touching and sexuality are opened and kept open—abusive sexual activity is confronted. The secrecy and denial integral to incest is eliminated. Responsibility for incest rests on the perpetrator. He has to apologize, be committed to maintaining a safe, non-abusive home, have a specific plan to prevent acting out, and a back-up system with negative consequences in case of a sexually abusive incident. Family therapy is not easy, but if done properly, recurrence of the incident is unlikely. The family confronts the painful reality of incest and each member (and the family unit) function in a healthy manner, not weighed down by stigma and secrecy.

GROUP THERAPY

What is the difference between self-help and therapy groups? Pundits say it's that therapy costs money. The group is led or co-led by professionals, deals with psychological complexity, is therapeutically focused, has strong norms about confidentiality, and is not social. Many people are in both self-help and therapy groups, and find the benefits from each quite different. This is especially true of time-limited, focused therapy groups.

Psychotherapy groups are broader ranging than self-help groups. The role of the therapist is to help members confront personal issues which are manifested in the group context of communication and relationships. People stay in therapy groups at least six months and often two years or more. One of the major differences between self-help and therapy groups is that, in the former, contacts between meetings (whether phone calls, social events, or a sponsor relationship) is strongly encouraged, while it is strongly discouraged in therapy groups. Dependency and identification as a victim is less a factor in psychotherapy groups.

Diane and Seth. Some couples meet through 12-step groups or recovery workshops. Although these relationships can work, they have special issues and problems. Relationships work best when each person has self-esteem—the relationship enhances each person's life and brings out the best in them. Too often, relationships serve as a problem-focused rescue effort. Respect, trust, and intimacy cannot grow in a victim-oriented relationship.

Diane and Seth met at a two-day workshop, "Finding and Loving Your Inner Child." There were over 300 people at this intense, emotional workshop. The leader was a guru in the best and worst sense of the word. She was dynamic and inspirational. Workshop exercises were powerful, with people expressing pain and shedding tears, and at the end experiencing feelings of euphoria and joy. Confronting shameful secrets, feeling pain, and overcoming it was empowering. The charismatic guru seemed so whole and healthy she inspired total confidence. All 300 people believed they could be healed. This optimism and openness brought Diane and Seth together. Discovering a cure for abuse and finding each other is the stuff of novels and movies. Diane and Seth felt like the luckiest, most special people in the world. The sex that they had the last night of the workshop was the most loving, passionate experience they'd ever had.

The first two weeks were golden. They had a marvelous time getting to know each other and listening to the guru's tapes. They cried about the past and exalted over their future. The problem with romantic love and golden dreams is that they soar very high and with equal intensity dive very low.

Diane's issues from her family of origin were feelings of insecurity, low self-esteem, and panic attacks. Her parents stayed married, but Diane grew up in a volatile, chaotic household. Father traveled a good deal and had a series of short affairs as well as two very disruptive love affairs. Mother reacted by being tearful and dejected, with occasional out-of-control incidents involving hitting and throwing objects. Diane was not physically or sexually abused, but did find Father a frightening person. He died when Diane was twenty-one and she remembers the wake and funeral as an extremely emotional and volatile event. There were fistfights severe enough to require police intervention. Mother's reactions ranged from heavy sobbing to anger at the "S.O.B." When Diane viewed the casket she too broke down sobbing. As the wake went on, she heard stories of Father from the strange people who showed up. She was ashamed to be associated with someone like him.

Mother had blamed all problems of life, marriage, and family on him. Diane hoped Mother would blossom with Father's death. However, Mother's life deteriorated. She obsessed about her ex-husband: Why he didn't have life insurance, how he dominated her, and how she hated being a widow at forty-seven. Diane realized Mother was a sad, ineffectual person who made demands on her children as a means of proving her worth and self-esteem.

Seth came from a dissimilar family, with different psychological issues, but felt equally deficit and vulnerable. Mother was clinically depressed through much of her life. Father was a workaholic, minimally involved with his family. Seth's family was financially secure with material comforts. However,

Seth felt unimportant and neglected. He had two younger siblings, but they'd never been close. When Seth returns to his parents' home for a holiday dinner, he is struck by how silent and emotionally empty the house is. People stay in their own world and purposefully avoid each other. When he was ten, Seth gave up trying to help Mother overcome depression. Her depression drove him away, causing her to feel guilty and more depressed. Seth used to eat and sleep at friends' houses to escape the deadly heaviness of his home. Although he'd never said this to anyone, Seth feared Mother would commit suicide.

As an adolescent and young adult, Seth acted out with drugs and sex. It gave him a feeling of being alive, and he ignored the risks. However, being arrested for a D.W.I. and losing his license for six months got his attention. Mother suggested seeing a psychiatrist, but Seth would have none of it—they'd been of no value to her.

The complex, difficult individual issues facing Diane and Seth were swept away by the high of the weekend workshop. The seductive message was: you can remake yourself into whoever you want to be. For people as needy as Seth and Diane, this answered their dream. Seth had a positive life message to drive him, and the joy of an energetic, loving partner. Diane's emotional interest and expressiveness were totally different from what he'd experienced from his mother and sister. The energy from a romantic, passionate sexual relationship was amazing. Diane was a bit less awed. She'd been in counseling during her two years at the state university so psychological awareness was not new. She hoped this time, however, it would last. Diane and Seth were buoyed by the workshop and were incredibly optimistic about their lives and relationship. The value of the guru's message was confrontation with secrets and pain, emotional catharsis, optimism about change—Diane and Seth felt the workshop had given them this and more.

The dangers of gurus and intense emotional experiences are they don't deliver on the changes they promise. Psychotherapists believe change is possible, and commitment and motivation are vital. It is crucial to have a change plan, implement it, monitor it, and be sure it remains successful (even though not perfect). Gurus ignore these elements, and so unfortunately did Diane and Seth.

Three months after the workshop, Diane and Seth were demoralized and their relationship was on its last legs. Diane felt Seth had betrayed her: he'd become angry and stubborn. Where was the sensitive man she'd met at the workshop? Seth felt abandoned. Where was the love and caring Diane had shown? They blamed each other, felt blamed, and blamed their parents—a strong theme in their Adult Child group. The motivation and hope they'd felt three months ago was gone. Although the 12-step group encouraged them to "nurture their inner child" and "work the program," it was too nebulous and didn't help.

As a last-ditch effort, they made an appointment with a therapist. In the four days between making the appointment and the session, Seth had gotten angry and left the apartment. Diane came alone, depressed and disillusioned. The relationship which had begun with so much hope and promise was a shambles. It is hard to revitalize this type of relationship and the therapist gave Diane the standard clinical advice. He told her she needed to work on her psychological understanding and personal issues before she could choose wisely and develop a viable relationship.

Diane found the psychotherapy process more difficult, less exciting, and more frustrating than the workshop or 12-step groups. She respected and trusted the therapist and believed he had her best interest in mind. She especially found the consistency helpful. In therapy, she did not back off examining painful, disappointing issues from the past or present. She missed the sense of excitement, charisma, and high she felt from the guru, but believed this approach offered lasting change. Therapy was hard, but when she saw Seth eight months later Diane felt she was an aware, healthy person.

Seth was impressed by her changes and eager to resume their relationship. Diane was flattered, but wary. She was able to realistically consider Seth, without the romantic glow. Seth's neediness was strong and Diane found it off-putting.

Seth was looking for a woman to rescue and take care of him. Diane felt Seth needed a therapist and she was looking for a life partner. She was tempted to use "Let's be friends," but knew it was difficult for ex-lovers to be friends. She resented what could have been.

Seth had reverted to a cynical way of analyzing the workshop and guru. Diane realized the workshop had been a waste of time, energy, and money, but found Seth's need to blame unattractive. Seth perpetuated his alienation by alienating others. If Diane and Seth tried to explore these issues, it would deteriorate into a defensive, accusing, counterattacking interchange. This realization made Diane sad, but reinforced her decision not to resume the relationship. She wrote Seth a short note, suggesting psychotherapy could be of value to him as it had been for her and wishing him good luck.

PSYCHOLOGICAL WELL-BEING VS. THE IDEALIZED LIFE

The concept of psychological well-being is useful for the large majority of people. The components of psychological well-being are self-esteem, quality relationships, competence and achievements, ability to deal with crisis and loss, and meaning and values. The person's attitudes, behavior, and emotions are congruent. External feedback is important, but personal understanding and goals take precedence. A person has multiple sources of self-esteem and is able to accept and integrate negative feedback and failures. Realism and self-acceptance are balanced with optimism and personally relevant goals. The past is accepted and dealt with, rather than denied or viewed as a source of shame. In the present, a person has a sense of pride and act in his best interest. He is not self-centered, but maintains nurturing, healthy, interdependent relationships. Feeling respected and cared for is important, as is promoting the well-being of others and the community.

When bad things happen, including events in the family of origin, a person is able to handle it in a problem-solving manner. One of the most, if not *the* most, important characteristics of psychological well-being is the ability to successfully deal with problems, crises, and loss. It is crucial for those with low self-esteem or from a dysfunctional family not to view a problem as an inevitable continuation of a family pattern. This approach repeats the childhood sense of victimization. Many adults do well for a time, but revert to a pessimistic mindset and feel like a helpless victim. A key to maintaining psychological well-being is to rationally assess and problem solve. At a minimum, a person returns to a state of equilibrium and, optimally, learns from the failure and develops superior coping skills. Pride in surviving a difficult experience promotes well-being. Psychologists use terms such as "the hardy personality," "psychological resilience," or "survivors" to describe this life approach.

Gurus and self-help books promise an idealized, problem-free existence after conquering trauma, addiction, or a dysfunctional family. Nothing could be further from the truth. The reality of human existence is that negative events occur to all people. Many difficult problems and crises can be avoided, some cannot. They have to be dealt with using appropriate coping mechanisms and resources. The most important resources are other people—trusted friends, family, professionals, a self-help group. Gurus are of little help, and often their teachings are destructive. They blame failure on the person for not strictly following their teaching on problem-free living. Psychotherapists do not promise problem-free living. They do suggest and teach healthy ways of thinking about and dealing with past and present problems. The message of psychotherapy is optimistic and hopeful—with changed cognitions, behavior, and emotional reactions, people can experience psychological well-being.

MAINTAINING AND ENHANCING LIFE GAINS

The first step in resolving a problem is to break through denial and confront the issue. This is the main contribution of the Adult Child movement—breaking the silence. In some ways this is the hardest step, in other ways the easiest. The next step is a careful assessment and understanding of the problem—how much of it lies in the past, how much in the present? Is it necessary to involve family or is it your responsibility to change? How you conceptualize the problem will heavily influence step three—intervention and change.

A little-discussed step is deciding you've made significant (not perfect) changes and need to maintain them. Maintaining progress in overcoming a problem—whether drinking, marital arguments, parenting, phobias, sex—is the most difficult part of the change process. Success depends on three things:

1. Setting reasonable (non-perfectionistic) goals.
2. When there is a setback or lapse, making sure it doesn't turn into a relapse.
3. Maintaining motivation and being accountable.

Ralph and Katharine. Ralph grew up in a family where Father hit Mother and the children. As an adolescent, Ralph had a reputation for a bad temper. However, Ralph swore he'd never hit his wife or children. He believed good intentions would be enough to ensure this. However, at twenty-nine, married five years to Katharine, with four-year-old and two-year-old daughters, the great hopes of five years ago were going downhill, especially since the birth of their last child. Ralph blamed Katharine for all problems and was full of resentment and anger. Katharine had grown increasingly afraid and alienated. They decided to enter couples therapy.

The prime goal of couples therapy was to prevent physical abuse. Ralph, however, set himself up for failure by setting perfectionistic goals of never getting angry and never spanking the children. He felt good intentions were enough and that he didn't need to learn anger management skills. When frustration and anger became overwhelming, he blamed Katharine rather than taking personal responsibility.

After a number of therapy sessions, Ralph developed a realistic intervention plan. He took responsibility by committing not to hit Katharine and if he spanked the children, to limit it to two spanks on the buttocks with an open hand. Katharine recognized her responsibility not to accelerate angry incidents, but instead to engage in emotional support and constructive problem solving.

Ralph designed a backup system to confront a lapse so it did not become an out-of-control relapse. If there was an incident, it was followed by a negative contingency dependent on the severity. For example, if he shoved or pushed Katharine, he would have to clean bathrooms for three months as well as formally apologize in front of the children. They had a written agreement that if there was an incident of beating (with closed fists or hitting with a chair), the police would be called and Katharine would file charges (previously, this had been a hollow threat hurled in the midst of a fight). Having a clear, written agreement made it more real.

Stopping physical abuse is not difficult, but maintaining a violence-free home is. When there are incidents or setbacks, how do you maintain motivation to stay with agreements and not revert to old patterns of impulsive anger, blaming, and violence? Positive motivation promotes maintenance of behavioral changes, especially pride in not falling into destructive patterns and having a healthier family of creation than your family of origin. Difficulties and lapses are confronted. Behavior, feelings, and perceptions are discussed, not distorted by guilt or shame. Good intentions are augmented by coping skills and an intervention plan. Therapeutic resources and self-help groups are available and utilized. Personal responsibility, accountability, and specific plans make the promise of change real.

CLOSING THOUGHTS

Hope and the advocacy of change is shared by gurus, self-help groups, books, and psychotherapists alike. All can make a positive contribution to the change process. Gurus raise public consciousness and provide hope that abuse will be confronted and resolved. They convey the message more effectively than scientists or therapists. Self-help groups reduce stigma, raise consciousness, and provide a structure and support for verbalizing secrets and addressing problems. For some, this is all that's needed to become a survivor. Many people, probably the majority, would benefit from professional therapy (as would their spouses and families). The therapy process recognizes and deals with the complexity, ambivalence, and individuality of issues from the past and present. The change process is usually bumpy and difficult rather than straightforward and easy. Therapy helps maintain motivation to deal with impasses and traps.

You deserve to establish and maintain changes in your life and family of creation. Use personal and external resources, especially psychotherapy, in getting where you want to be in life.

13
BEING A SURVIVOR—LIVING IN
THE PRESENT

Often people say, "Being a survivor, not a victim, sounds so right and so easy, why can't I do it?" It is a goal worth reaching, and people deserve to reach it, but it requires time, psychological energy, use of multiple resources, and good luck. Gaining and maintaining psychological well-being is not easy, no matter what pop psychology gurus, books, and TV talk shows say.

The most important guideline is living in the present with positive anticipation and goals for the future.

Harriet and Art. Harriet had been ritualistically tortured from ages eight to eleven by a brother who was five years older. The brother later became an intravenous drug user and was dying of AIDS. Harriet's husband, Art, felt the brother had caused Harriet such pain that she owed him nothing. Harriet agreed she didn't owe it to him, but needed to consider whether she wanted to see him. She had written a letter to her parents outlining the abuse, telling them she was in therapy, and asking for their understanding and acknowledgment. She'd had several conversations with her mother, an important conversation with her father, and they'd attended a family therapy

187

session when in town for a visit. Harriet was clear about the abuse and felt validated by the reactions of her parents and Art.

After discussions in therapy and with her women's support group, Harriet decided to contact her brother. She wrote a letter, stating resentment about the childhood abuse, sadness he was suffering from AIDS, and asking if he wanted to see her and meet her children. The brother had not contacted Harriet in over three years. He'd joined an AIDS support group where they urged him to get his affairs (practical and emotional) in order, including making amends to people he'd hurt. He wrote to Harriet, asking to see her and meet her children. He was too weak to travel, and Harriet asked Art to accompany her on the visit. She needed Art's emotional support and help with the children.

Harriet was shocked to see the brother. Physically, he was much weaker than she expected. Emotionally, he was more open than at any time in his life. He told Harriet that at thirteen he had become involved in a drug-based, satanic cult group. His ritualistic abuse of her stemmed from this. He was tearful in his apology and assured her the abuse wasn't a response to anything she'd done. Harriet did not trust his deathbed confession nor did she like the "born again" quality of his fervor, but believed he was genuinely sorry. He met her oldest son. Harriet left that meeting with sadness about her brother's life and impending death. She was relieved he'd apologized, she'd accepted the apology, and felt at peace with herself and her past. Everything wasn't "okay," but the abuse had been dealt with in a healthy manner. Art demonstrated he was there for Harriet, which increased her self-esteem. Harriet felt like an adult survivor who deserved a respectful, loving life.

THE PSYCHOLOGICAL HEALING PROCESS

The process of healing is complex, primarily psychological (although it can have a spiritual component), and is ongoing, encompassing awareness of sensitive and vulnerable areas. Healing begins with an attitudinal and emotional acceptance of the complex reality of abusive childhood experiences. It includes acknowledging positive experiences which gives perspective to a painful childhood. Healing also includes the ability to view parents as people with strengths and weaknesses. Psychological healing involves using resources—therapy, self-help groups, books, spouse, best friends, minister, parents, or siblings—to increase understanding and acceptance. Most of all, it entails a focus on the present, a commitment to being a survivor who deserves to act in his best interest. Healing involves putting thought, time, and psychological energy into developing loving, nurturing relationships. It means incorporating into the present elements of the past you value and being aware of traps to monitor and not repeat. Psychological healing is an ongoing process; you cannot rest on your laurels.

Exercise—How Far You've Come, What You Need to Do

This exercise involves writing and then sharing the material with your spouse, best friend, therapist, or self-help group. You'll need a pen and two pieces of paper. This will take a good deal of thought and might require two or more sittings.

On the first paper list insights, activities, and learning you've achieved thus far in the journey from being a victim to a survivor. Examples could include telling your spouse or friends painful childhood stories, reading a book or article that shows you are not alone in dealing with abusive experiences, having a talk with a parent or other relative to learn more about your childhood and family, attending an Adult Children of Alcoholics group for eight months, taking a ten-session class on effective parenting, writing a letter (which you need not send) to the person who abused you, allowing yourself to cry over missed opportunities of childhood, making a commitment to having a more respectful, intimate marriage than your parents, discussing feelings of guilt with your pastor and heeding his advice that God wants you to be healed, reading a self-help book, going to a church-sponsored family weekend retreat, attending twenty sessions of individual psychotherapy. List at least three things you've done to build self-esteem and become a survivor.

On the second paper list issues, feelings, and concerns (traps) that continue to block the healing process. Be as specific as possible. Examples might include feeling tearful or angry whenever you think of the abusive situation, when something negative happens feeling it is tied to the old problem and will never change, continuing to abuse alcohol or engage in out-of-control gambling, engaging in self-recrimination about the abuse, blaming everything on the past and indulging in self-pity, spending so much time and energy going to 12-step groups that your job and relationships suffer, obsessing on how you hate the abuser, feeling your life is mired in the recovery process, reading two self-help books a week and getting discouraged because you're not as healthy as the case examples, not being able to talk to siblings without re-fighting old battles, feeling like a confused, second-class person, avoiding relationships because you don't want to be hurt again.

Now that you've listed one to five traps, beside each write one or more coping strategies. Examples could be to set aside "quality" time for yourself and your family, focus on solving one problem at a time rather than trying to change five things at once, choose the self-help group that is most helpful and drop participation in others, interact with family members who are supportive and maintain distant contact with others, find a therapist or minister who respects you and treats you like a first-class person, when you feel sorry for yourself do something active that affirms your personal worth and power, set realistic goals, write out alternatives and problem solve, when obsessed with anger from the past realize you did survive, practice effective expression of feelings.

The next step is to design a system to utilize your coping strategies and ask your spouse or best friend to encourage you. It takes practice and effort to stop falling into self-defeating traps.

LIVING IN THE PRESENT

Living in the present and planning for and anticipating the future sounds easier than it is. When something goes wrong or there's negative feedback, it's almost a reflex action to feel that's the way things were, that's the way they'll always be, and it's the fault of your childhood and dysfunctional family. It is disheartening when the same problems repeat themselves and easy to conclude things will never change. That depressing trap is neither true nor is it in your best interest.

Living in the present includes being aware of vulnerabilities and traps from the past. Knowledge is power. Awareness of problems is a crucial first step. If you get stuck at that step, you will revictimize yourself by becoming demoralized and act out self-defeating patterns. Living in the present is a commitment to being active, involved, and responsible. Insight and awareness are necessary, but not sufficient, for change. There needs to be a commitment to goals which are in your best interest, a strategy or change plan to reach those goals, a problem-solving approach to implementing change, with special attention to monitoring progress and not getting thrown off track by failures or negative feedback.

A man with three young children was acutely aware of his family history of violence. He was strongly committed to not repeating that pattern with his children. However, he would become very upset and scream at them. They would become frightened and cry and he'd feel terrible. Although he did not engage in physical abuse, his outbursts upset the children. He felt like an emotionally abusive father, and questioned whether the family would be better with him out of the house. Children do deserve to live in a safe home. If Father cannot control abusive behavior, then his leaving would be the right option. This man loved his children and desired to be a good parent. The key was to avoid physical abuse and focus on reducing the frequency and intensity of anger and verbal abuse. This was a reasonable goal which he could achieve. When there was an angry incident, rather than berating himself and giving up, he viewed it as a lapse. He did not minimize, but examined why the incident started, what caused it to accelerate, and assessed the severity of verbal abuse. He apologized to his wife and children. Angry feelings are normal, but acting out those feelings in an abusive manner is not acceptable. He was committed to have a healthy family and entered therapy to learn anger management skills. He knew it was a vulnerable area and he wouldn't be perfect, but needed to significantly improve. His goal was to reduce the frequency and intensity of angry incidents and be a nurturing, loving parent.

Focusing on the present holds you accountable. You cannot hide behind the screen of victimization. Awareness of dysfunction and vulnerability from the past can empower and motivate in the present. Use insights as resources for change, not excuses for why you can't change. For example, those from alcoholic backgrounds should either abstain from drinking or carefully monitor and moderate their drinking. It is easy to fall into the trap of repeating the past—if you come from a physically abusive family, to have an abusive marriage and family; if you come from an alcoholic family, to marry an alcoholic or become alcoholic; if you were sexually abused as a child, to have a family where sexuality is a "hot, unspoken issue" or where sexual abuse is repeated. Living a respectful life means being aware of and monitoring traps. You need to devote time and psychological energy; that is a legacy of a dysfunctional family. It means not indulging in obsessing about the past, fantasizing about changing the past, or seeking revenge. You need energy to focus on the present.

FEELING RESPONSIBLE

Saying "I can do it" or "I'm responsible for myself" are pop-psychology adages that are true, but simplistic. The reality is that change requires much thought and effort. The psychological adage of taking an active, involved, responsible stance is easier said than done. The extreme stance "you can be anything you want to be" is untrue and self-defeating. Establishing a genuine sense of responsibility means accepting one's strengths and weaknesses, one's potential for personal growth as well as vulnerabilities and problem areas. It means setting realistic goals where you have a good chance of success, not unrealistic goals where you become demoralized by failure or pretend to be someone and something you're not.

An example of someone who is self-defeating because he has set unrealistic goals for himself is the man who grew up in a financially strained, dysfunctional family and feels it's crucial to his self-esteem that he becomes wealthy. He feels cheated by an unsuccessful attempt to "hit it big" and is unrealistically optimistic about his new business or investment opportunity. Earning a reasonable income and being financially responsible is an important component of psychological well-being. In most instances there is a direct relationship between skills, effort, and financial payoff. Set realistic goals and realize you attain financial success based on reality parameters rather than seeking the "big hit" or the "financial miracle." Betting food money on the lottery is not a sign of responsible planning.

Establish personally meaningful goals rather than striving for status or approval of others. Many people, especially in job, financial, and housing decisions, go with "conventional wisdom" rather than evaluating individual needs. Examples include choosing to work for a larger, more prestigious company rather than the smaller, well-run company with a collegial atmosphere; buying a home in the "trendy" neighborhood rather than a well-built house in a pretty, friendly community; sending your child to the "right" music teacher rather than the teacher whom your child likes and is motivated to work with. Get information, weigh alternatives, and then make the choice which best meets your needs and values. Learn to respect your "gut feelings."

An example of a person who is not acting in her own self-interest, but is still caught up in reacting to a dysfunctional family of origin, is the woman whose parents were obsessive-compulsive, very frightened of taking any action or making any decision. She was determined not to repeat that pattern and went to the opposite extreme of making impulsive decisions, many of which backfired. Adults who overreact to parents' problems get into as much trouble as those who repeat

194 CONFRONTING THE VICTIM ROLE

the parental pattern. Be less reactive to your family of origin, focus on your needs and goals. If you become obsessed by trying to undo the past or repair family of origin damage, you don't have time or energy to focus on your life, relationships, and family.

Some adults take the position that unless issues with the family of origin are resolved and the pain of the past alleviated, they will cut off contact. Using that criterion, 90% of families would cease contact. This would be to the detriment of grandparents, adult children, and children. Only in the exceptional case is the clinical recommendation to cut off family contact. If maintaining contact results in ongoing victimization, the harsh reality is that stopping contact is the healthiest alternative. Don't make that decision without professional consultation.

The usual guideline is to maintain family contact, but within reality parameters. Establish realistic expectations and don't expect a reversal or making up for the past. Being responsible includes being sure your children are not abused by their grandparents or extended family. It means being a more aware, protective parent than your parents.

A PERSONAL NOTE.
Our children very much benefited from contact with Emily's family, especially her parents. However, we stayed alert for incidents of violence, which did occur on an intermittent basis. We told our children if a physical incident began they were to get us. If we were not available, they were to go to another room; it was not their responsibility to take care of the problem. However, if there was blood or Grandmother was on the ground and couldn't get up, they were to go for help. We told Emily's parents about these instructions. Knowing this was the situation reduced the incidents of violence when our children were present. This was a harsh reality to address in a responsible manner, but since it was the reality, it had to be faced and dealt with in an imperfect way. This was better than pretending

there wasn't a problem or demanding a perfect resolution which was not possible.

Gina and Ward. Gina and Ward met in their early thirties and married two years later. This was Gina's second marriage and Ward's first. Gina had married at eighteen, hoping to escape an alcoholic, chaotic family. Negative motivation seldom promotes positive behavior, and this proved true of Gina's marital choice. She had two children in rapid succession. Two months after the birth of the second child, Gina's husband was arrested for driving while intoxicated. He did not live up to the requirements of his probation and was incarcerated for thirty days. At that point, Gina decided she'd had enough of his irresponsible behavior. Although wary of being a divorced mother with two young children, she knew it was better than being trapped in a fatally flawed marriage.

Female-headed families with young children are vulnerable to poverty and a host of dysfunctional problems. At twenty-four, Gina was determined her life and the lives of her children would not fall into that trap. She did several things to promote her family's welfare. Gina joined an Adult Children of Alcoholics group and attended regularly for ten months. When she left the group it was with a feeling she had learned a great deal about herself and alcoholic families and was ready to move on. She joined an informal support group of single mothers with children. It was at one of those meetings she heard about a state program to fund education and training for single mothers. It took a great deal of follow-through, assertiveness, and arranging of practical details, but Gina successfully completed a three-year hospital-based nursing program. She worked weekends as a hospital nurse and was a part-time college student, completing her B.A.

Gina reestablished a relationship with her family of origin. She wanted her children to know their grandparents, uncles, aunts, and cousins. She had realistic expectations about her parents; she knew she could not force Father to confront his alcoholism or change Mother's passivity/depression. They were better grandparents than parents. An unexpected bonus was the help and concern from her brother and sister-in-law. They became her personal cheering section and the cousins were very close—Gina was glad her children had a sense of family.

Ward was a successful industrial engineer who was adept at solving organizational problems and promoting efficiency and morale. He was an analytic person, good at listening to employees' complaints, problem solving, and introducing changes that made the system work better. Ward was well respected and well liked by both colleagues and management. He was a gregarious fellow who participated in the office softball league, organized birthday parties, and arranged group lunches. Ward did little dating and was not comfortable in one-on-one situations. The more personal the conversation, the more anxious Ward became.

Ward's secret was he had been sexually abused by a stepsister who was six years older. In most male's minds, an eighteen-year-old girl sexually initiating a twelve-year-old boy would be a dream come true, not abuse. It's frightening how sexual myths so pervade our culture. The essence of sexual abuse is that the older, more powerful person uses a younger, more vulnerable person to meet sexual needs. In the great majority of cases, it is the male who perpetrates sexual abuse—this is true whether the victim is female or male. Yet, there are females who are sexually abusive.

Ward looks back on those incidents extending over two years as a devastating and humiliating experience. The abuse involved a range of sexual activities, but centered on his performing cunnilingus, with her being critical and ridiculing. Since he became erect and ejaculated, he must have enjoyed the experience. So how could it be abusive? He was silent about these experiences, sharing them with no one. It was Ward's "shameful secret." As an adult he kept emotional distance from his family of origin. He behaved correctly and was cordial, even with his stepsister.

Ward did not trust women and was very unsure of himself

sexually. He had occasional intercourse-focused affairs with minimal affection or foreplay. His longest relationship had been fourteen months, but the woman lived in another town and they only saw each other on weekends.

Ward met Gina when he was the assistant coach of a baseball team on which Gina's son played. Ward had a positive influence on the boy, improving skills and, more importantly, increasing his confidence. Gina was grateful and admired Ward's easy way with children. In turn, Ward was impressed by what an involved parent Gina was. When he heard of the struggle to complete her education while working and raising two children, he knew Gina was a woman worthy of respect. They didn't date the first year, but did a number of group activities. They would exchange hugs and back rubs, but didn't kiss.

Gina did not enjoy the dating scene. When Gina was twenty-five, a divorced woman in her fifties shared advice that stuck with her—"You're better having a lover than a series of affairs." Gina had had "lover" relationships that lasted anywhere from one to four years. She found the relationships sexually fulfilling—sex was something Gina valued, one of the pleasures in her life. However, she did not pretend these relationships were better than they really were. She had not met anyone she would want to share her life with, and one of her goals was to remarry and have a baby.

It was Gina who made the move to romanticize her friendship with Ward. She found Ward attractive and wanted to pursue an intimate relationship. She was taken aback by Ward's intercourse focus, but perceived this as nothing more than his masculine style. Gina's friends were happy for her and, for the first time, her kids liked the man in her life. Ward cared for Gina and enjoyed being sexual, but was worried. Gina wanted more from the relationship, both emotionally and sexually, than he could give. Ward feared if Gina learned of the sexual abuse, she would no longer love and respect him. Ward had to protect himself and his secret. He was attracted to marriage, Gina's family, and the idea of having a baby. Their eventual decision to marry was greeted with enthusiastic support by friends, colleagues, and neighbors.

Gina and Ward talked about the important and hard issues that are so crucial for successful marriages, especially with a blended family. They discussed finances, parenting, housing, religion, raising two adolescents and having a baby, friendships, danger of affairs, couple time, and developing a respectful, trusting, and equitable bond. They ignored two areas—family of origin and sexual intimacy. Gina and Ward colluded in not discussing these sensitive topics. These can't be ignored, and as the wedding got closer, conflicts appeared.

Gina couldn't understand Ward's distant relationship with his family and was frustrated by his verbal and non-verbal message: "Don't talk about this." Gina was concerned that her family behave appropriately at the wedding. She especially worried about alcohol consumption and the possibility of a fight. Ward was forthcoming with suggestions and backup plans for which Gina was grateful.

Ward stopped sexual initiations, and Gina resented always having to initiate. Her feelings were hurt when he said "no" as he did with increasing frequency. Gina was feeling less attractive and missed being sexually desired. She did not discuss this, naively hoping it would improve after marriage. Instead, sexual activity practically ceased. When they entered couples therapy three years later, they had not had intercourse for almost two years. They both, however, wanted to have a child.

After an initial couple session, Gina and Ward were scheduled for individual history taking. Gina discussed family of origin issues and legacies. The therapist made several suggestions, including not having secrets from a spouse and the importance of establishing a vital marital bond. Gina discussed these issues with Ward, especially family secrets and her desire to deal with things directly rather than allowing them to fester as they had in her family of origin. Ward was supportive and receptive when dealing with her family; however, he did not self-disclose about his family.

Ward canceled his individual appointment twice. When he did appear, he was inordinately anxious. The therapist began by saying most people had sexual secrets and if therapy was to be helpful they would need to understand the sensitive, negative, and/or traumatic incidents from Ward's past. He assured Ward these incidents would not be disclosed without Ward's permission. In the sexual history, Ward revealed little until asked, "In looking back on your childhood and adolescence, what was the most confusing, guilt-inducing, negative, or traumatic occurrence?" As Ward began discussing the sexual incidents with the stepsister he broke down and, between the sobs and guilt, couldn't finish. The therapist suggested Ward write notes about the incidents—when they occurred, where, what happened, how often, and what he was thinking and feeling at the time. Another session was scheduled, and then four more sessions where Ward explored in detail his thoughts, experiences, and feelings about the abuse. Ward's shame had multiplied over time. A trap in keeping abuse secret is that the incidents become more powerful and distorted. After discussing the advisability of doing so, Ward shared memories and feelings about the abusive incidents with Gina. This opened a new level of communication. Gina understood Ward's reticence to cope with sexuality. She was empathic and supportive in dealing with his trauma. She wanted to develop an intimate relationship and have Ward trust her as a sexual friend and spouse.

Sex therapy is not easy or problem free, but Gina and Ward were excellent clients. They respected and liked each other and wanted an intimate marriage. Ward was able to confront sexual guilt and pain from the past, and feel supported by Gina, not blamed. They wanted to build a sexual bond and conceive a baby. When they experienced an inhibition or anxiety, they handled it as an intimate team without blaming or turning on each other.

Ward felt vulnerable if touching did not immediately proceed to intercourse. Non-demand pleasuring was anxiety provoking. He needed to be aware of vulnerable feelings and deal with them rather than becoming frightened and avoidant. Although Gina enjoyed cunnilingus, she realized this was too difficult for Ward and agreed it was not to be part of their sexual repertoire. As Ward challenged sexual anxieties, trusted

Gina's concern for his feelings, and enjoyed her sexual respon-
siveness, his inhibition began to subside. Ward told Gina how
important it was for her to be personal (as opposed to intellec-
tual or analytic) when talking about their sexual relationship.
The big breakthrough occurred when Gina became pregnant.
Both were ecstatic. Ward believed Gina would be totally involved with the pregnancy and want to keep sexual distance.
Gina felt just the opposite; it had taken two to create this baby
and Gina wanted Ward's involvement throughout. He went
with her to the obstetrician, attended childbirth classes, and
joined a prenatal education group.

Gina desired to maintain intimate touching. During the first
trimester, she had more than morning sickness, she felt nau-
seous all day. Although not desirous of intercourse, she continued to be interested in giving and receiving non-demand
touching. The second trimester was more sexually active. As
her stomach got larger in the last trimester, they switched
intercourse positions to side-rear entry and sitting-kneeling.
More important than technique was the need to maintain emotional and sexual intimacy. For the first time, Ward felt like a
complete man—husband, father, and lover, involved in an
intimate relationship with no secrets. Gina was proud of herself
and of her family.

YOU DON'T HAVE TO BE PERFECT
TO BE A SURVIVOR

One of the biggest problems with recovery stories or self-
help books is that they portray people too perfectly. People's
lives, families, and relationships are more individualistic and
complex than portrayed by abstract theories or simplistic slo-
gans. A person can be a survivor even though her life and
relationships are not perfect. The key element is taking personal responsibility. Accepting deficits from childhood and
family of origin is a necessary step in the process. This can be
done without feeling stigmatized or burdened, even if the past
was severely abusive and traumatic. Accept strengths and
weaknesses, hopes and vulnerabilities, experiencing self-es-

teem that incorporates the pain and satisfactions of who she is and who she is becoming.

Recently, the child development and parenting literature has emphasized the concept of the "good-enough parent" rather than the "all-knowing, totally loving, perfect parent." When people set unrealistic, perfectionistic goals, they condemn themselves to feeling inadequate and insecure. If your expectation is to be the perfect adult, always responsible, totally loving, totally self-accepting, these unrealistic expectations create a self-fulfilling prophecy of never reaching your expectation. It's normal to have resentment and hurt from the past—it doesn't totally go away no matter how much therapy or how many 12-step groups you attend. It's normal in the present to occasionally be anxious, frustrated, or depressed—that's part of the human condition. Hurts and disappointments need not be blamed on the past or be seen as playing out the victim role.

A mother who has a conflict with her adolescent son should not blame this on coming from an alcoholic family or predict her son will become alcoholic. The feeling of helplessness and predestination is not based in reality. This sense of revictimization and repeating patterns of the past is the opposite of feeling and acting like a survivor. Mother does need to deal with being raised in an alcoholic family. However, that cannot define how she parents her son; if it does, it will be to her detriment and hinder his development. She needs to understand her background and concern about alcoholism. Since almost all adolescents experiment with drinking, it's unlikely there is anything she can do that will ensure he not try drinking. She can make him aware of the family's vulnerability to alcohol abuse (whether she believes it's genetic or learned), and the importance of monitoring drinking. She needs to deal with her son and his drinking for what it is, not as a symbol of her father's alcoholism. She can use resources—spouse, good friends, professionals she respects—to provide feedback and advice on parenting.

Each person desires to be respected and treated as an individual; this is especially true of adolescents. One of the pitfalls of adolescence is lack of a sense of history and balance. It's easy for the adolescent to take an oppositional stance. In this case, the son is more likely to do this if he sees his mother so wrapped up in the past that she doesn't have the energy and concern to parent him and deal with his concerns and problems. Both mother and son have to focus on present issues.

CLOSING THOUGHTS

The crucial message is the importance of being a survivor and living in the present. This is not a simplistic cliché. As we tried to show with exercises, case illustrations, guidelines, and short examples, being a survivor is a complex process with few perfect resolutions. Is it worth it? Absolutely. The freedom and awareness to act in your best interest is a source of pride. Instead of feeling devalued by the past, destined to feel victimized and revictimized in the future, you can be a survivor who builds a life of responsibility, caring for yourself and others. Self-respect and self-esteem are central. Accept the complex reality of your past and use this awareness to empower you to lead a loving, successful life. Victims wallow in a self-defeating, self-focused world controlled by the past. Survivors focus on achieving a balance of personal responsibility and caring for others. They neither deny the past nor feel controlled by it. They live fully in the present and plan for the future.

14
PSYCHOLOGICAL WELL-BEING

Life is to be lived in the present, with planning and anticipation of the future, not controlled by the trauma and demons of the past. The adult deserves to live a responsible, loving life, not just for herself, but for her children. The challenge is to live one's life as a healthy survivor, overcoming the victim role, to feel genuine pride in not repeating patterns of abuse and dysfunction, and being a better parent than one's parents. This can't start with parenting. It needs to start with oneself, with self-esteem as a survivor.

Psychological well-being begins with the individual. The most nurturing, consistent parents are those who take care of themselves. In traditional families, males and females had very disparate lives and sources of self-esteem. For females, the main source was caring for others, especially children. For males, it was career success and money. Adults need multiple sources of self-esteem. Both males and females gain self-esteem from personal achievements, quality relationships, career successes, money, coping with adversity, community or religious activities, personal maturity, learning a skill or sport, overcoming a handicap, being competent and assertive, enjoying a new experience. Men and women are better parents when their personal lives are functional.

The most important relationship in a family is the husband-wife bond. When the parents are doing well (both as individual people and a couple) it is likely they will be effective parents. Adults who ignore individual well-being and marriage and focus only on the children are not acting in the long-term best interest of their family. It is not in the child's best interest for adults to live through their children; children need to develop their lives, not compensate for adult insecurities or shortcomings.

Parenting is time and energy consuming and is one of the most challenging and rewarding life experiences. Parents commit to providing a stable child-rearing environment. Three guidelines are: 1) being consistently nurturing and supportive, 2) practicing parenting behavior which is clear and predictable, 3) viewing the children's needs as more important than the parents' emotions (i.e., parents don't take their anger or depression out on children). Adults who grew up in dysfunctional families did not have this type of parenting. They can improve by taking parenting classes or consciously working with their spouses to implement this style of parenting. Good parenting is not instinctive—it's a learned set of attitudes, skills, and emotional responses.

The adult who takes care of himself, is competent and caring, establishes a satisfying and secure marriage, and is a nurturing, consistent parent, can feel proud. He is acting in his best interest and in the interest of his family by overcoming the cycle of abuse and dysfunction. The core is being a responsible, loving adult—thinking and acting like a survivor. Psychological well-being is not a function of age, but increased awareness, personal responsibility, capacity to trust and love, acting in your best interest, and nurturing others.

Paula. Paula had seen three therapists, been in two psychotherapy groups, and four 12-step groups. She was twenty-seven, twice divorced, and had a four-year-old daughter, Susan. Paula identified herself as an Adult Child of Alcoholics (both parents) and victim of incest (her father sexually abused her). Paula had the self-esteem of a victim and acted out that role. She began to see a fourth therapist.

Paula was acutely aware of abuse and dysfunction in her family of origin. When her siblings got together they shared family horror stories. Father died seven years ago of a heart attack, and three years later Mother died of liver failure. Their deaths and funerals were highly emotional and volatile. Other than recognizing family dysfunction, Paula had done little to retake control of her life. Identifying and feeling the pain of abuse is a necessary first step in becoming a survivor, but as Paula vividly demonstrated, if you stop there you are stuck in the victim role.

Paula found therapy this time frustrating and difficult. The sympathy she had come to expect from therapists and group members was not forthcoming. The therapist acknowledged her pain, was respectful and empathic, but confronted her about using insights and feelings in the present. Paula rebelled and said he was asking too much, especially concerning depression and parenting. Paula recalled traumatic incidents at age four and said she needed to heal *her* four-year-old before she could attend to her daughter's needs. The therapist told Paula that she could not recapture her childhood. No matter what pop psychology books say, it *is* too late for a happy childhood. It is not too late, however, to be a loving, responsible person and a nurturing parent. Paula could take pride in Susan's healthy development.

Paula had three dreams she believed, if they came true, would make her life perfect. She fantasized a wealthy man would fall in love with her and take care of her and Susan; she dreamed of a different family and childhood; and she longed for friends/support community who would totally be there for her. These unrealistic fantasies left Paula frustrated and hopeless—leading to continued feelings of victimization. Paula needed to set personally meaningful, realistic goals that she had a good chance of reaching.

Instead of expending angry energy, Paula needed to accept the harsh reality that her ex-husband was not going to provide child support. Her work as a practical nurse would not generate sufficient income. She would either have to enter an R.N. program or switch careers. Paula decided on the latter and received on-the-job training as a computer technician—a sought-after, well-paying skill that has recently attracted female applicants.

Through Susan's preschool, Paula learned of a parenting class for single mothers sponsored by the county adult education department. She learned new attitudes and skills and developed two friendships. One of these was with a woman who had grown up in a neglectful family and the other was with a woman from a well-functioning blended family. These women accepted Paula and, with mutual encouragement, the effectiveness and satisfaction of all three as parents increased. They shared stories about the past as well as hopes and plans for the future. They talked about relationships and sex in an honest, helpful manner. They made fun (in a nice way) of Paula's "Cinderella fantasy" of the wealthy man who would rescue her and allow her to live like a princess. Men could bring strengths to a relationship, but also brought their weaknesses and problems. One woman told a story of a friend who married for money and in the five years of marriage and subsequent bitter divorce felt she'd earned every penny.

Paula was then determined not to marry a man who would cause pain and disappointment, no matter how rich or attractive. She stopped looking for a man to rescue her and adopted the attitude that it would take a special man and relationship before she'd remarry. Paula would need to believe the bond of respect, trust, and intimacy was solid so they could handle the special challenges of a blended family. The man would need to respect her, not be attracted by her weaknesses. Paula wanted a life partner and equitable relationship.

Sexually, Paula had two gears. At the beginning of the relationship she was very interested, giving, and experimental. She joked, "I have some of the best meaningless sex around." As the romantic glow dimmed and Paula realized the man's faults, her disappointment was expressed sexually. Desire dramatically decreased and criticalness dramatically increased.

The therapist felt Paula had to deal with her incestuous history. Incest is a personal and sexual betrayal. The perpetrator (in over 90% of cases a male) puts his sexual needs above the needs and feelings of the child (in over 80% the incest victim is female). Incest is three times more frequent in alcoholic families.

Paula was profoundly ambivalent about sexuality. She experienced desire and orgasm only at the beginning of the relationship and when she was drinking. Sex was functional, but Paula didn't really "own" it—arousal came from the newness, romantic love, and alcohol haze. Paula functioned sexually better than most incest victims, but did not consider sexuality a positive, integral part of her.

In counseling incest survivors the adage "living well is the best revenge" is particularly relevant. Paula needed to identify sex as being good, sexuality as an integral part of herself as a woman, and express sexuality so it enhanced her life and intimate relationship. Concretely, that meant Paula would no longer be swept away by romantic love or use alcohol to remove inhibitions. These are not healthy sources of sexuality. Paula agreed to have no more than two drinks before sex. She insisted the man use condoms to prevent sexually transmitted diseases and the H.I.V. virus. She conscientiously used a diaphragm.

Paula had learned that sex equaled love, so she had to believe she was in love in order to feel sexual. She became disappointed and critical when it turned out this wasn't the ultimate relationship.

Paula had read a slew of self-help books—about why women chose badly, were co-dependent, loved too much, chose Peter Pan types, how to find the right man. She talked ad nauseam about this in groups and with friends. When she was attracted to a man, she was swept away by passion, intensity, and romantic love. The idea of being comfortable and communicative with a man you were passionately in love with seemed incongruous. Sex/passion was on a totally different dimension than comfort/friendship. Paula was struck by how unrealistic her model of choosing men had been. She was a romanticist and sex drove the romanticism. Reality caused disappointment and an explosive breakup.

It's easier to assess past problems and traps than focus on developing healthy relationships. Paula needed to feel comfortable, develop a quality friendship, and communicate emotional and sexual feelings. She felt more aware and confident about her judgment in choosing a man and understanding relationships. Paula eventually wanted an intimate, secure marriage, but realized this was not the present reality.

A legacy of Paula's childhood was feeling emotionally needy, bordering on desperation. Using sex to prove she was lovable and worthwhile was part of a self-defeating cycle. The therapeutic focus was improving self-esteem, increasing competence as a mother, acknowledging achievements, improving career skills, and building a circle of friends (females, males, and couples) who liked and respected her. This was not easy, nor was it a "magic formula for happiness." It did provide multiple sources of self-esteem and life balance. Paula had looked to a man to give her self-worth. The basis of self-esteem is personal; it cannot depend on another person or external sources.

Paula's romantic relationships ceased being destructive, but continued to be disappointing. She still felt less respect for the man after six months than at the beginning of the relationship. During the year and a half of therapy, she'd fallen in love and contemplated marrying three different men. Intellectually, she knew this was dysfunctional, but her emotional needs overrode rationality. The therapist's tack was he didn't want to waste therapy sessions discussing the man until she'd been in a relationship at least three months and respect and quality were growing. No relationship met those criteria.

Paula had grown a great deal during therapy. She dealt with the pain of an alcoholic family and incest. She'd rebuilt relationships with siblings and two aunts, and sadly decided to maintain emotional distance from one abusive brother. Paula was a responsible, nurturing parent and Susan was thriving. Paula continued to have financial difficulties, but managed money responsibly. Her career and friendships were growing and gave her a sense of pride. Yet, Paula felt like a failure because she had not established an intimate relationship.

Finding the right person to marry is *not* a reasonable goal for therapy, nor a measure of self-esteem. The self-help market preys on people, specifically women, promoting the idea that they're not married or married to the wrong person because of family-of-origin problems or not confronting personal flaws. If she does what the book or self-help group advocates, she will find happiness and sexual fulfillment with Mr. Right—an unrealistic promise, which, when it doesn't happen, causes the woman to blame herself (or the male gender) and feel like a victim.

The therapist urged Paula to acknowledge gains and continue to act in ways that improved the quality of her life. She remained open to an intimate relationship, but realized she could maintain self-esteem and psychological well-being without a man in her life. Paula was involved with people and activities she enjoyed rather than expending time and energy in the frustrating pursuit of a man.

Regular therapy sessions were terminated and a six-month follow-up session scheduled. At that session, Paula was actively involved in three community groups and proud of her life and parenting. She continued to be disappointed about, but accepted, not having an intimate relationship.

Eight months later she called for an appointment to discuss the concept of a sexual friend. Paula's concern was whether a relationship which had not begun as a hot, passionate affair could turn into a quality intimate relationship. The therapist expressed his belief that a quality relationship could indeed ensue and gave examples of couples with comfortable, respectful, trusting relationships who had developed a satisfying couple sexual style. Paula continued to monitor traps and keep her life on track. Two years later the therapist was pleased to receive a note announcing Paula had married and that the bond of respect, trust, and intimacy was solid.

Children from abusive, addictive, or dysfunctional families have impaired psychological well-being. However, it is possible to develop a responsible, loving, satisfying adult life. There is no "easy, magic key."

Self-esteem is the core of psychological well-being. You are not born with self-esteem; it develops from life experiences, especially family, school, and people interactions. It is crucial to view yourself as a survivor, not a victim. Develop personal responsibility: don't be controlled by guilt, anger, or sadness about the past. Psychological well-being involves healthy, loving relationships. You are not a rock or an island; you need people for a sense of community, continuity, and support. Closer, special relationships, where you feel accepted for who you are, are especially valuable. Be involved with people and groups who support healthy, functional behavior. An intimate, secure marriage is a boon to psychological well-being.

Psychological well-being is based on competence and achievements, not a "feel-good" approach to life.

Almost anyone can maintain psychological well-being when everything goes well. The reality of the human condition, however, is that negative experiences, conflicts, and losses happen. Accepting and coping with negative events (both present and past) is of paramount importance to continued psychological well-being. No one has a problem-free existence. The crucial difference between psychologically healthy and problematic people is their willingness and ability to cope with negative experiences and crises. Being able to accept hard realities and cope is integral to psychological well-being. Acute crises and problems are easier to face because when you successfully deal with them you return to a positive equilibrium. Chronic problems are more of a drain. Don't be a passive victim; be sure the problem doesn't control you. People can and do live with chronic problems while maintaining psychological well-being.

Meaning and values vary for individuals. It is crucial to have a personally meaningful, stable framework that gives value to your life. Human beings need to believe in something more than themselves and the feelings of the moment. Neither psychotherapy nor the recovery movement is a substitute for spiritual or religious values.

There is a difference between functioning and well-being. Being a survivor and functional adult is necessary, but not sufficient, for psychological well-being. Life satisfaction is a process with unique characteristics for each person. It involves a positive balance between external and internal factors and an integration of attitudes, behavior, and feelings. It includes feelings of pride, joy, commitment, connection, and love. People from dysfunctional and abusive childhoods not only can survive, but can thrive, establishing self-esteem as a responsible, loving person. They develop psychological well-being and convey this to their family of creation.

Exercise—Establishing Psychological Well-Being

The focus of this exercise is to examine the five component areas of psychological well-being: self-esteem, quality relationships, competence and achievements, coping with crisis and loss, and meaning and values. What changes do you need to make in order to attain psychological well-being?

The format is to take five pieces of paper (one for each content area) and divide each into three columns. In the first column list vulnerabilities and areas to monitor from childhood; in the second column, attitudinal and behavioral skills you need as an adult to be a functional survivor; in the third column, plans, hopes, experiences, and emotions to be a loving, responsible, satisfied adult.

For example, under competence and achievements in the first column one might list as vulnerabilities: being called stupid by Father; being an angry, acting-out adolescent who was an underachiever; and having poor models for adult functioning. In the second column: acknowledge being intelligent; pride in work; being an involved parent; and saving money for a down payment on a house. In the third column: strive to master one's job and/or set up his own business; refurbish his home; establish an intimate marriage; be a nurturing, consistent parent; a mentor for students or apprentices; and a board member of a community improvement group. Examples under relationships in the first column would be: physically and sexually abused by older brother; feeling dependent on friends for self-esteem; trying to save parents' marriage by getting flowers for Mother and saying Father sent them. In column two: feeling responsible for self; aware of self-defeating habits and relationships; acknowledge self as a sexual woman; establish relationships where she is respected and liked, but doesn't feel dependent. The third column: establish a strong personal identity; develop an intimate, secure marriage; be a good educator and resource for her children; have three close same-sex friendships and two couple friendships: and keep clear boundaries with family of origin.

Be aware of your unique personal characteristics and goals—don't answer in a socially desirable manner or pretend something which is not true. Psychological well-being is a very individualistic concept; people organize life components differently. There is not "one right way to be happy"; there are many paths. Being a responsible, loving person requires more than good intentions. Identify traps from the past so they don't control your adult life. "Pay your dues"—change attitudes, behavior, and emotions. Identify what you personally value and set realistic goals to attain psychological well-being for yourself and your family.

THE DIFFERENCE BETWEEN
AGE AND MATURITY

When you're young, adults tell you things will get better as you "mature." Research indicates adolescence and young adulthood (to age twenty-five) are the most difficult and unhappy times in people's lives. Major changes and transitions— even planned, healthy ones—can be disruptive. Life experiences facilitate the maturing process. Forty-one-year-olds have more experiences and can put things in perspective better than twenty-one-year-olds. However, it's not age or experience alone that cause maturity. It's the ability to be self-reflective and learn from experiences. The mature person is aware, responsible, and a good decision maker.

A key is learning to assess issues and be a competent problem solver. By this definition, there are plenty of fifty-year-olds who are immature and some very mature twenty-five-year-olds. Being a healthy adult doesn't come with age, but with an increased sense of awareness, personal responsibility, and capacity to trust and love. The mature person is aware who deserves trust (and who doesn't?) and maintains clear personal boundaries.

Paul. Traditionally, males denied abuse or minimized the effects of abusive experiences. Paul was the middle of three sons who grew up in a family where Father was a compulsive gambler with a series of different jobs and extramarital affairs. Father was a hard-working, competent carpenter who would not take orders from superintendents. When things went well he was well liked and considered a good worker, but if he lost at gambling, had a blowup with his girlfriend, a fight with his wife, or was angry at his sons, everything could explode. He blamed others and wouldn't take personal responsibility. He abandoned his family when the oldest son was six, Paul was four, and the baby two. Mother was a consistent caretaker, but depressed. She managed a laundromat, a low-paying but steady job. She never dated after her husband left; she had no interest in men or sex. Paul was not sure whether his parents were ever officially divorced. Her life was her sons. She loved the role of mother and homemaker. Friends enjoyed visiting the house because there were always snacks and they weren't hassled. She encouraged studies, athletic participation, and church attendance.

After high school, Paul's older brother entered the Navy and made it a career. He married, had two children, and lived overseas. Although they continued pro forma contact, Paul did not feel close to this brother. The younger brother went to college for two years, but dropped out. His career involved sales, and he often changed jobs, looking for bigger commissions. He'd been married twice—once for two years and once for three. He had one child for whom he made child support payments, but had little contact. However, the grandmother was very involved with her grandchild. This brother was now involved in the men's movement—going to weekends in the woods five or six times a year.

Paul finished college with a major in architecture. His area of expertise was rehabilitating houses in city neighborhoods. Paul was very involved in his community with good friendships and strong roots. He married at twenty-nine, the last of his brothers to marry. Three years later he had a daughter; two years after that, a son, and then a vasectomy. Paul had a satisfying relationship with his wife, Bonnie, who worked as an attorney for a state agency. Paul thought of his family of creation as five people. He included Mother, who was the children's regular child care person.

The year before Father died, Paul visited him in New Mexico. Father had been glad to see Paul and hear news of his children and grandchildren. Father did not give explanations or apologies (this was not his style), but said he was not the kind of man who should have married or had children. He joked that the first thing he'd done after leaving was to get a vasectomy. He confirmed Paul's mother and he had never divorced—this was a perfect reason to give if a woman wanted to marry. Father had a better life in the West, and did not regret leaving.

Paul had mixed feelings about the visit. He wanted to be a different person than Father, especially to maintain an intimate marriage and be a consistent, nurturing parent. Paul found Father very interesting, with many of the characteristics he both liked and disliked in his younger brother (the brother was offended by the comparison because he conceptualized his involvement in the men's movement as searching for his lost father). Paul talked extensively to Bonnie about the visit. Paul trusted Bonnie and was not inhibited in sharing discoveries, concerns, insights, and ambivalence. Paul did not feel a need to share details with Mother, which was fine with her. Paul did discuss the visit with his children, and they enjoyed hearing stories of their grandfather.

Paul and Bonnie attended couples therapy for seven months. This was not in response to a crisis, but Paul's desire to strengthen parenting skills and emotional and sexual intimacy.

Family-of-origin material was discussed in individual sessions and shared and processed in couple sessions. Especially important was Bonnie's desire to be seen by Paul as the primary parent, not his mother. Paul did not want to be in the middle between Bonnie and Mother (who had a good relationship). Paul's reassurance of Mother's worth and how integral she was to the family was more disrupting than helpful. Paul realized he was overcompensating for his childhood. He needed to accept that not everything would be perfect. He had a life, marriage, and five-person family he could enjoy and be proud of.

Although Paul had been a sexually interested man, he'd reduced his initiations considerably since they'd had children. Bonnie's initiations were hesitant and tentative because she didn't want to be perceived as putting pressure on Paul. Discussion of initiation patterns and couple sexual exercises increased comfort and reenergized sexuality. Both became adept at initiating, making requests for alternative pleasuring scenarios rather than saying no, and increasing affectionate touching both inside and outside the bedroom. In Paul's view of Bonnie as a mother, he had denied her sexuality. Bonnie's increased acceptance of herself as a sexual woman as well as a mother proved a powerful turn-on for Paul.

Change did not cease when therapy terminated. Paul was committed to living his life as a loving, responsible person in an intimate, secure marriage and having a healthy, nurturing family of creation. Paul and Bonnie were willing to invest the time and psychological energy to follow through and make this a reality. When hard issues emerged, they dealt with them. Paul wished he'd come from a healthier family, that his mother had more of a life, and his brothers were more functional; but he didn't impose his wishes on others. He took pride in his life and enjoyed feelings of psychological well-being.

CLOSING THOUGHTS

We hope this book, with its guidelines, case examples, and exercises, has convinced you that people from abusive

backgrounds and dysfunctional families can and do have loving, responsible lives and attain psychological well-being. It
is not an easy task—and, yes, victimization in childhood is a
significant handicap. The more pervasive and severe the abuse
and the more lacking in compensations, nurturing, and predictable life experiences, the more the person will need to utilize
professional and self-help resources to deal with the pain of
the past and keep his/her life on a healthy track. Experiences
of childhood are accepted rather than denied and are not the
determinants of self-definition. The goal is to live in the present
as a survivor who accepts the challenge to develop a healthy,
satisfying life and family of creation.

Psychological well-being is not a nirvana state that only an
elite minority attain. Psychological well-being involves developing attitudes, behavior, and emotional responses which are
congruent and healthy. There is a positive balance among
component areas of self-esteem, quality relationships, competence and achievements, coping with crisis and loss, and meaning and values. It is unrealistic to expect that you or anyone will
be optimally functional in all areas. Being a loving, responsible
adult means establishing personally relevant, reasonable,
achievable goals, not striving for perfection. All people have
weaknesses and areas of vulnerability.

Psychological well-being involves being an optimistic person who can meet the challenge of confronting an abusive
childhood, seeing yourself as a survivor, and thriving as a
loving, responsible adult who builds a satisfying life and
healthy family of creation. Good luck on the journey.

APPENDIX I
CHOOSING A THERAPIST AND
SELF-HELP GROUP

As stated from the outset, this is not a do-it-yourself therapy book. People are reluctant to consult a psychotherapist, feeling that to do so is a sign of "craziness" or failure. Seeking professional help, however, is a sign of psychological strength. Entering individual, marital, group, or family therapy means you realize there is a problem and you've made a commitment to being a survivor and attaining psychological well-being.

The mental health field is confusing. Psychotherapy is offered by several types of professionals including psychologists, social workers, marriage therapists, psychiatrists, sex therapists, and pastoral counselors. The background of the practitioner is of less importance than her competency in dealing with your specific problem. It is important to choose a therapist who is aware of abuse and family-of-origin issues.

Many people have health insurance that provides coverage for mental health and thus can afford the services of a private practitioner. Those who do not have either the financial resources or insurance could consider a city or county mental health clinic, a university or medical school mental health outpatient clinic, or a family services center. Clinics usually have a sliding-fee scale—that is, the fee is based on your ability to pay.

In choosing a therapist be assertive in asking about credentials and areas of expertise. Ask the clinician how long therapy can be expected to last and whether there is a focus on communication, problem solving, family of origin, or family of creation. Ask how he feels about issues of victimization and his experiences with 12-step programs. A competent therapist will be open to discussing these issues. Be especially diligent in questioning credentials, such as university degrees and licenses, of people who call themselves personal counselors, adult child counselors, marriage counselors, or sex counselors, since there are poorly qualified persons—and some outright quacks—in any field.

One of the best resources for obtaining a referral is to call a local professional organization such as a psychological association, marriage and family therapy association, mental health association, or mental health clinic. You can ask for a referral from a family physician, minister, or friend who has information on a therapist's areas of competence.

If you have a problem that principally concerns marriage or family issues, you could write the American Association for Marriage and Family Therapy, 1100 17th Street NW, 10th Floor, Washington, D.C. 20036, for a list of certified marriage and family therapists in your area. If you are experiencing a sexual problem, you can write the American Association of Sex Educators, Counselors, and Therapists, Suite 1717, 435 N. Michigan Avenue, Chicago, IL 60611, for a list of certified sex therapists in your area.

Feel free to talk with two or three therapists before deciding on one with whom to work. Be aware of how comfortable you feel with the therapist, the degree of rapport, and whether the therapist's assessment of the problem and approach to treatment make sense to you. Once you begin therapy, give it a chance to be helpful. There are few "miracle cures." Change requires commitment and is a gradual and often difficult process. Although people can benefit from short-term therapy (less than ten sessions), most people find the therapeutic process will take at least six months to a year. The role of the therapist is that of a consultant rather than a decision maker. Therapy helps change attitudes, feelings, and behavior, which improves self-esteem and relationships. Be sure the therapist is aware of your goal to live your life as a survivor and to confront the victim role. Chapter 12 contains more information on the therapy process.

SELF-HELP GROUPS

Psychotherapy and self-help groups can be complementary. There are strengths in self-help groups which surpass the benefits available through psychotherapy. It is crucial to choose a group which focuses on your specific problem. Being in a group with people of similar backgrounds and problems reduces stigma and lets you know you're not alone. The group provides an accepting milieu that reduces shame and secrecy which is so destructive to self-esteem. The group provides a steady, consistent source of support. Group members who succeed in changing their lives provide a positive model and source of learning. Having a sponsor to give guidance and support can be of particular benefit. In the group, the person learns new attitudes, skills, and ways to healthily express emotions.

Here are guidelines to consider: 1) choose a group that has a tradition of stability and success; 2) be sure the group is focused and small enough; 3) be sure there is a solid cadre of sponsors; 4) choose a sponsor who respects your needs; 5) be sure the group will allow you to cut back or leave without coercion. Chapter 11 provides more information on the use and misuse of self-help groups.

Neither psychotherapy nor self-help groups are panaceas. When 12-step programs (or psychotherapy) reinforce the sense of victimization, these interventions are harmful. Ideally, psychotherapy and self-help groups would be complementary in helping the person confront the secrecy and shame of an abusive childhood, see herself as a survivor not a victim, live a life of self-esteem, and establish a healthy and satisfying family of creation. The confrontation and change process is difficult, but worthwhile. Change is facilitated when the person uses all

available positive resources—therapy, books, groups, programs, sponsors, friends, relatives. Be aware of negative
sources that keep you stuck in the victim role—these include
unethical or incompetent professionals, books that give bad
advice and overpromise, groups that allow members to wallow
in anger or self-pity, and programs that go nowhere or are
inappropriate for your problem. Choose the type of therapy
and/or self-help group which promotes healing and psychological well-being.

APPENDIX II
BOOKS FOR FURTHER READING

Alberti, Robert, and Michael Emmons, *Your Perfect Right.*
(Sixth Edition). San Luis Obispo, California: Impact Publishers, 1990.

Bass, Ellen, and Louise Thornton. *I Never Told Anyone.* New
York: Harper Perennial, 1991.

Burns, David. *Feeling Good.* New York: Signet Books, 1980.

Earle, Ralph, and Gregory Crow. *Lonely All the Time.* New
York: Simon and Schuster, 1989.

Hazeldon Foundation. *The Twelve Steps of Alcoholics Anonymous.* New York: Harper and Row, 1987.

Kaminer, Wendy. *I'm Dysfunctional, You're Dysfunctional.*
Reading, Massachusetts: Addison-Wesley, 1992.

Lehner, Harriet. *The Dance of Anger.* New York: Harper and
Row, 1985.

Lehner, Harriet. *The Dance of Intimacy.* New York: Harper
and Row, 1989.

Lew, Mike. *Victims No Longer.* New York: HarperCollins,
1990.

Maltz, Wendy. *The Sexual Healing Journey.* New York:
HarperCollins, 1991.

McCarthy, Barry. *Male Sexual Awareness.* New York: Carroll
and Graf, 1988.

McCarthy, Barry, and Emily McCarthy. *Sexual Awareness*. New York: Carroll and Graf, 1984.

———. *Female Sexual Awareness*. New York: Carroll and Graf, 1989.

———. *Couple Sexual Awareness*. New York: Carroll and Graf, 1990.

———. *Intimate Marriage*. New York: Carroll and Graf, 1992.

Peck, Scott. *The Road Less Traveled*. New York: Simon and Schuster, 1978.

Seligman, Martin. *Learned Optimism*. New York: Pocket Books, 1988.

Tavris, Carol. *Anger: The Misunderstood Emotion*. New York: Touchstone Books, 1989.

Wolitz, Janet. *Adult Children of Alcoholics*. Deerfield Beach, Florida: Health Communications, 1990.

———. *Healthy Parenting*. New York: Simon and Schuster, 1991.

Woolfolk, Robert, and Frank Richardson. *Stress, Sanity, and Survival*. New York: Signet Books, 1979.

Other books available by Barry and Emily McCarthy from Carroll & Graf

"No matter who reads them, they'll be getting the best books in the crowded sex-ed field. The McCarthys are knowledgeable, tolerant and practical—qualities that give their efforts great authority."
—ALA *Booklist*

COUPLE SEXUAL AWARENESS $9.95
This book is written for people who wish to enhance their sexual life and overcome problems that often undermine stable and satisfying relationships.

FEMALE SEXUAL AWARENESS $9.95
Here is book about women and how they can enhance their sense of sexual identity by emphasizing a pleasure-oriented approach to intimacy.

INTIMATE MARRIAGE $10.95
The McCarthys explore the complex relationship of marriage, clarifying and examining issues crucial to women and men whether married or single.

MALE SEXUAL AWARENESS by Barry McCarthy $9.95
The focus here is on both single men and men as part of a couple. It explains why men feel and believe as they do; and it offers practical, helpful advice for men and their partners so they can achieve fully integrated, rewarding sexual lives.

SEXUAL AWARENESS $9.95
This book shows individuals and couples how to improve their sexual pleasure. It is focused on feelings and fulfillment.

Available from fine bookstores everywhere or use this coupon for ordering.

Carroll & Graf Publishers, Inc., 260 Fifth Avenue, N.Y., N.Y. 10001

Please send me the books I have checked above. I am enclosing $_____ (please add $1.25 per title to cover postage and handling.) Send check or money order—no cash or C.O.D.'s please. N.Y. residents please add 8¼% sales tax. Canadian residents please send a Canadian Postal money order or a check drawn on a U.S. Bank, **In U.S. Currency.**

Mr/Mrs/Ms _____

Address _____

City _____ State/Zip _____

Please allow four to six weeks for delivery.